Travels w'

Int

KEN &

Do you remember were formed and shaped when you took you. grandchildren or perhaps great grandchildren on family vacations? Remember the memories that were fashioned when events didn't unfold as planned? Stories told around a good meal served at a crowded table of family and friends still bring laughter and smiles. At each telling the stories improve in stature as each generation adds their interpretation.

Grandpa [Ken], Grandma [Bonnie], and their children; Renee and Jeff. The story teller's of their generation

From ages six and eight, travel with the boys across the wilderness regions of Michigan's Upper Peninsula to the asphalt paths of the Grand Canyon's Rim trail at ages ten and twelve. Join the Dickson's as they experienced the northern wilderness and the arid southwest from the perspective of their grandkids.

Why Can't I Roller Blade in the Grand Canyon will bring your own family's memories back to life. Every family has those memories tucked away, and typically they are brought to life once or twice a year when families and friends gather together around a packed dinner table. With just a little prodding or perhaps with a lull in the conversation the family's story teller will gather everyone together with *"Do you remember the time…."*

Relive those funny moments of youth that are common to every family and those moments that weren't humorous at the moment, but upon reflection …. Were some of the best times.

Bonnie and I have come to the conclusion that we were truly blessed by their company. SPECIAL THANKS TO: **Zach, Taylor, Trevor, Kenneth, Derrick, Adrianna, Renee, Jeff, Fred, Dan, Wendy, and Doug & Sue. Thanks for the great memories, and….**

For the realization that life is the journey not the destination.

In the Summer of 1994 Zachary was 6. Known as Zach to his buddies, he had just completed kindergarten, one of the first milestones of his youth, and was eagerly anticipating the other adventures that awaited summer and his entrance into first grade. His stature among the neighborhood boys had greatly increased as word spread of the bloody "robin's nest" incident and the resulting seven stitches. On the other hand, emergency room physicians still recount the time when Zach tried to imitate Evil Knievel by jumping over his first BMX bike on roller blades.

Taylor and Zach during the Summer of 1994.

Taylor was 4 in the Summer of 1994 and following the antics of his older brother and mentor was not only a badge of courage but a challenge. Taylor claimed responsibility for the infamous second

Why can't I roller blade in the Grand Canyon ?

floor clothes chute and their cat Pierre, but in their defense they did place sheets and pillow cases in the basement hamper.

Taylor and Zach at Marblehead Lighthouse.

The Woods' family annals still list Taylor's rear deck hockey incident as number one in comparison to their red plastic two-man loge and the elaborate glass mirror at the foot of the staircase. But the reader can make their own decision.

With the loge increasing speed, Taylor settled into the reddish plastic sled's lead position as the boys left the crest of the stairway, as the last obstacle in clearing the second floor staircase loomed

Why can't I roller blade in the Grand Canyon ?

into view as they headed for the front door and success. The hard right turn failed to materialize as they crashed into the full length ornate glass mirror leaving hand and face prints on the shattered glass as visual reminders of what could have been.

The hockey game turned out to be an individual sport. Resplendent in all the latest safety equipment, Taylor took the wooden deck like he owned the arena. The score was nothing to nothing as Taylor took a hard check to the wooden rail, crashed down the steps to the concrete drive way, managing to knock out his two front teeth with the end of his hockey stick before scoring the winning goal.

Taylor at Wampler's Lake.   Zach at Wampler's Lake

Figuring that nothing else could go wrong, we decided that the boys were ready for their first camping adventure away from home and more importantly away from Mom and Dad.

Why can't I roller blade in the Grand Canyon ?

At that time, our camping gear consisted of a J. C. Higgin's camping trailer with the original canvas that my parents bought from Sears & Roebuck in 1958, and sold to us in 1974. Each of the four compartments would hold four heavy cardboard beer boxes that we used for food, can goods, clothes, and other necessary camping gear. You should have seen the looks we would get from other campers when we unloaded the Higgins and all those beer cases would come tumbling out.

J.C.Higgin's camping trailer, Great Grandma Dickson, and the Dickson's 57 Ford Ranch Wagon.

With two new tires and wheels in place and the best mounted as a spare, Zach and Taylor have declared the camping trailer's maintenance finished, and therefore confirmed the camping season was officially opened. We told them that they would be the first to go camping in the trailer as soon as spring arrived, and according to them, every weekend is camping weather.

Plans were made using the first nice weekend before school let out for the year, the spare beer box was packed with their clothes, and the Higgins was attached to the Jeep. It's only about an hour's drive to Walter J. Hayes State Park, and when the boys asked me how much longer I always replied "two minutes."

Why can't I roller blade in the Grand Canyon ?

After setting up camp and demolishing the McDonald's hamburgers that we purchased in Tecumseh, Bonnie decided that a walk to the beach and its playground was just the thing to round out the first night. After giving the boys my standard answer of "two minutes" to their oft repeated question of "how much longer," we arrived at the beach. With all the rain that has visited the Irish Hills this spring, Hayes was alive with flowers and we were even able to get in a lesson on flowers when we found a whole hillside of white trillium in bloom. When Taylor asked the name of those white flowers, Zach replied "petals of three, or was that leaves of three, I can't remember, its either a white trillium or poison ivy." What I weekend this is going to be.

Taylor and Zach swimming at Wampler's Lake.

In case the boys got homesick we made arrangements with Renee and her husband that they would drive up just in time for lunch on Saturday, spend the afternoon, and leave before dinner. So we were not surprised when Renee said; "Dad, the boys want to go home," and with that simple statement our first camping adventure with our two oldest grandsons was coming to an end, less than a day after it had started.

Why can't I roller blade in the Grand Canyon ?

For the first day out with the boys things aren't going to bad. We had hoped to get an early start, but as usual what can go wrong will go wrong, and it will always occur at the last minute. We finally got on the road about 9:45 am and we couldn't have been down the road 5 feet before I remembered that I hadn't put on the towing mirrors. At about the same time Bonnie remembered that she had some bills to post. Both tasks were taken care of in Samaria, it's a good thing it was on the way.

Lunch break at Lake Fanny Hooe, Michigan's Upper Peninsula.

We had one heck of a head wind and ended up driving most of the way in 3rd gear, instead of overdrive. The temperature was in the high 90's with humidity to match. The car ran great till we got to the

Why can't I roller blade in the Grand Canyon ?

incline on I-75 just past West Branch. I guess trying to keep it at 65 was just too much. The car didn't overheat but the "Check Engine" light came on and stayed that way till we pulled into Hartwick Pines. While Bonnie went to register, I checked under the hood and everything looked like it was in its proper place. Anyway when I restarted the engine it had clicked off and hasn't come back on. Maybe it was just to hot......who knows.

We got into the "Pines" and it wasn't long before we had the camp squared away. Even though it was at least 95 degrees Taylor wanted to start a fire right away. He finally settled for playing catch with Zach in the empty camp next to us. There was a slight swale between the camp-sites that was bridged by a fallen tree. Of course this was just to good to pass up and it wasn't long before both of them had fallen off. No broken bones just a few more bruises.

"Where's lunch? Hartwick Pines Michigan.

Why can't I roller blade in the Grand Canyon ?

Travels with the Grandkids
Ten days in the North Woods, Summer 1995

I have forgotten how much two small boys need to inspect the bathrooms. All of the public facilities between Toledo and Grayling have passed their critiques.

The afternoon was extremely hot and we passed the time visiting several friends in the area. We thought that Jack and Madge Bender's place on Lake Margaret would be a good place for the kids to swim and cool off. K-Mart provided the boys with a new softball, which they tried out in the backseat of the car on the way to the fish hatchery, incidentally, the hatchery was a great learning experience.

The trip from Hartwick Pines to the Soo is 148 miles, or a little under 3 hours driving time. But if you listen to the boys it was 154 minutes of unrelenting boredom with nothing to do except ..... stop at every possible restroom, and then drink more water so that they can do it all over again.

We drove over to Norton's place at the Neebish Island ferry. It's a good thing we hadn't planned on staying at their place because they didn't have the camp-sites in yet. Pat made a real hit with the boys by giving them each a box of cookies with their milk. For them it was a great snack, so then they did what comes naturally to young boys, they slept all the way back to Mission Point.

Zach and I char-broiled the pork chops while Bonnie and Taylor pealed the potatoes and shucked the corn, just kidding, they used a can opener, and we ended the meal with peaches. About 9:30 pm after numerous games of running catch, and several bathroom inspections, it was finally time for bed. Bonnie and I have forgotten just how much work two young boys are. Well I know I have, Bonnie just has this all-knowing smile. It's 9:53 pm and we have just gotten them to bed, and we are still looking for the off button. The day cooled off perfectly and we were lulled to sleep by the snapping and cracking of the Airstream's aluminum skin as it contracted in the evening air.

We are camped at Mission Point on the bend of the St.Mary's River

Why can't I roller blade in the Grand Canyon ?

and it is a perfect place to throw stones. With boys being boys the admonition to stay out of the water means absolutely nothing. Several soakers later, I caught Taylor walking in the water. So when I yelled at him to get out of the water, he told me that Zach said he could do it. Taylor later got even with Zach. As you are aware a four year old who is going on 16 does not have a good sense of direction when it comes to throwing stones. Well one of his perfectly aimed boulders caught Zach in the middle of the back. And of course Zach played the wounded martyr bit to the hilt.

Zach and Taylor at Mission Point on the St. Mary's River.

This morning's breakfast was an interesting lesson in diplomacy. Our scrambled eggs and bacon seems to be the hit of the younger crowd. However, those two boys know exactly how many pieces of bacon are contained on each of their plates. Taylor can't count past

Why can't I roller blade in the Grand Canyon ?

ten but he knew that Zach had 6 more bacon pieces.

According to Zach we passed through Paradise 15 minutes ahead of schedule. They were both trying to read the map, when both of them, one in each ear, spotted and announced the sign to Andrus Lake. We were able to get the last available campsite on the water, and the boys were out of the car in a flash. The trailer was barely disconnected from the car before they were on the beach shoeless. I have never seen two boys remove their shoes and socks on the run before, and then stop one thousandth of an inch from the waters edge. Bonnie and I checked out the waters depth, set their limits, and then watched them have the time of their life. I thought that 20 minutes would be the limit of their endurance to the cold water and I was off by three minutes. They both came out of the water telling each other that it was to cold for swimming, and hollering for towels. About the time the goose pimples faded so did their memories of the cold water and they were at it again. Boy, did they have fun.

Zach, Taylor, and Grandma at Whitefish Point.

Why can't I roller blade in the Grand Canyon ?

We just finished dinner and the boys have really had a full day. They could swim when ever they wanted to and they wanted to three times. Getting back to what I wanted to tell you was that during dinner they were both so tired, Bonnie and I thought there were several moments when they were going to bury their faces in the noodles. At the moment they are doing the dishes, Zach's washing, and Taylor .... well, I think he's drying.

Zach and Taylor with the evening's campfire and marshmallows.

Why can't I roller blade in the Grand Canyon ?

Once again Taylor knew that Zach had five more pieces of bacon in his scrambled eggs. I still haven't figured out how he knows this but it was true.

After breakfast we wrote out several postcards and dropped them off in Paradise on the way to the Upper & Lower Tahquamenon Falls. I thought that it would be a good idea to start our tour of the falls by 9 am so that we could beat the crowds. We were about 30 minutes late, but the logic was flawless.

Tahquamenon Falls and the rowing crew.

Bonnie and I remembered what we didn't like about the Upper Falls as we were coming back up the 94 steps from the observation platform at the edge of the falls. Zach has one heck of a memory; he remembered a scene from "Last of The Mohicans" when they were hiding out behind the falls, and then related that scene to the

Why can't I roller blade in the Grand Canyon ?

fact that he could see behind the root beer colored waterfall. His eyes are pretty good too, because he spotted another observation platform down-river and said "let's go to that one too".

Campsite at Andrus Lake with the Jeep and the Silver Bullet.

We tried to dissuade him from the other platform by telling him we couldn't find the trail. Zach went up to this guy in uniform who was supervising a group of workers in striped uniforms and asked him if he knew the way to the other platform, and the guy just pointed down the trail. Well, that one has 124 steps, and several long inclines.

We got back to Andrus Lake in time for what I thought was a much deserved rest, but as usual Zach and Taylor thought it was time to go swimming. Lunch was postponed for about 20 minutes. That's just about how long it takes for them to discover that the water is cold.

Feeding the geese at Andrus Lake.

Just after our lunch, mother goose and her four charges came for their lunch also. We made the mistake of feeding them yesterday and now we are considered a regular campground meal stop. Armed with two pieces of bread each, they stood on the edge of the water and tossed the bite size pieces to their wards. Trouble erupted when the bread ran out before their ward's appetites were satisfied. The geese's behavior became way to aggressive for the boys, so they slowly retreated up the bank towards the safety of the trailer and Grandma, followed by the four peepers and mother goose. We spent most of the afternoon watching the boys turn blue and then thaw-out. After our three o'clock tea and cookie break we piled into the car and headed for Whitefish Point. The boys had been after us the whole trip to let them go swimming in Lake Superior. We told them just how cold the water is and that even their mom and Uncle Jeffie hadn't dared to go swimming in that cold lake. Well they wouldn't be persuaded, and as they ran

Why can't I roller blade in the Grand Canyon ?

towards the lake their shoes and socks were being tossed aside. It's the first time this whole trip that they thought it was too cold to go swimming, and all they had to do was to put both feet in the water.

Tea and cookie break Andrus Lake.

What a night! Taylor has posted a new record for falling out of bed....three times. I'm not quite sure how he accomplishes the feat, especially when he lands on the floor on his rear and totally out of his sleeping bag. Perhaps he has some help from Zach. Both of them occupy the front settee which folds out into a double bed. Zach being older has taken first choice and has opted to be against the wall, Taylor, well he's taken what's left. Our last night at Andrus Lake was filled with swimming and a trip out to Vermillion Life

Why can't I roller blade in the Grand Canyon ?

Saving Station.

The 9.2 mile road to Vermillion would test the patience of a saint, of which I don't even come close. The boys learned several new phrases when we encountered a ditch that someone had dug across the dirt/gravel road. The boys just giggled at my out-burst, and I knew that they were planning on trying those out on their parents at some opportune time, and then blaming the whole thing on Poppa.

The road to the Station and the Vermillion Life Saving Station.

Why can't I roller blade in the Grand Canyon ?

We couldn't go down to the beach at Vermillion because of the nesting Plover birds. According to the caretakers they only had 17 nesting pairs returning to the area this year. We had hoped to see a lot of deer on our journey to and from the station and the boys were really disappointed.

After the boys and the geese had breakfast we packed up the rig and headed south for the Straits State Park. We had planned on meeting with Renee and Dan at noon and we wanted to be a little early. The journey to the straits takes a little over an hour and just outside of Trout Lake we had to make a panic stop to avoid hitting a fawn and its mother. Once the boys heard the tires squealing their heads came up from whatever they were doing and watched us narrowly miss the deer.

We couldn't believe the scene in St. Ignace when we arrived. The approaches, exit ramps, and clover leafs were jammed with motor homes, trailers, tents, and other means of camping. People were everywhere, and it was only Friday morning the first day of a three day car show..

We made our way to the campground and site number 284. While Zach and I set up the trailer, Bonnie and Taylor got the lunch together. Renee and Dan hadn't arrived yet, so we decided to spend the afternoon visiting friends that run a couple of unique shops. When we arrived back at the campground, Renee and Dan had arrived, and the boys were really glad to see them after almost a week of grandparents.

After dinner we rounded up the boys, and with our lawn chairs and blankets, we headed for Main Street to enjoy the cars that cruise up and down the strip. By 9 pm Bonnie and I headed back to the trailer and called it a day.

Renee and Dan have opted to stay another day with us at the Straits and I think that I'm happier than the boys. After lunch we piled into the Jeep and headed for the Cut River Bridge. Once

Why can't I roller blade in the Grand Canyon ?

again Zach and Taylor found the path leading out of the picnic area to the beach adjacent to the Cut River and Lake Michigan. The stairs at Tahquamenon Falls have nothing on the steps at the Cut River Bridge. According to Zach's count there are 215, but Taylor only came up with 47, however his counting system has more ins and outs than "new math".

After the stairs at the Tahquamenon Falls.

Sand bars have built up near the beach where the Cut River empties into Lake Michigan, and if you're careful and use the

Why can't I roller blade in the Grand Canyon ?

proper boulders you can make it from one side of the river to the other. Grandpa was very careful and provided an excellent example of river hopping. Zach and Taylor made it to the first boulder and then promptly fell off. They continued the journey by foregoing the rest of the boulders and wading the rest of the way through the cold waters of the Cut River. The boys compared the temperature of the clear water to that of Lake Superior. It's been a long time since Bonnie and I had been under the Cut River Bridge, but we did recall a path leading directly under the bridge and coming up into the rear of the picnic grounds. We found the path, and we were soon standing directly under the bridge. The path to the picnic grounds was rather steep and the climb really tired out us older people.

Zach, Taylor, Dan, Renee, and Grandma at the Cut River Bridge.

After several rounds of refreshing water from the jug we keep in the back of the car, and several Oreo "Double Stuff" cookies, Zach and

Why can't I roller blade in the Grand Canyon ?

Taylor had sufficiently revived to walk to the middle of the Cut River Bridge. Once we arrived in the exact center we had to practice our marksmanship by squirting mouthfuls of water over the bridge railings into the Cut River, 528 feet below. I scored a direct hit, while Zach and Taylor need more work. The day cooled off perfectly and we were once again lulled to sleep by the snapping and cracking of the Airstream's aluminum skin as it contracted in the evening air.

Cut River Bridge.

The boys left for home early Monday morning with their parents in a light rain. The weather forecaster felt that the rest of the week would be engulfed in afternoon thunder-showers; so far he's been correct. We left early Tuesday in a heavy downpour after a night of lightning and thunder.

We had a great time!

Why can't I roller blade in the Grand Canyon ?

Bonnie had the trailer packed and the Jeep positioned so I could hook up when I got home Friday. Zach and Taylor came right from school, and they were ready to go. As a matter of fact, Taylor was waiting at the end of the drive, so that he could alert the other members of the entourage when I arrived.

"He's here, and I am not kidding this time," Taylor shouted reminding the neighbors of Peter and the wolf. I wondered how many false alarms he was responsible for, especially since Bowsher High School had a false fire alarm a couple of hours ago. I was trying to work out the logistics of the false alarm when Bonnie opened the door to help me with my brief-case and thermos.

Within minutes the trailer was hooked up, kids buckled up, house locked, and my cup of coffee placed on the console. A quick check of the trailer and car found an errant electrical connection that Zach had failed to detect. With all the hustle and bustle of the afternoon, the electrical connection was overlooked. We all turned to look at Zach, who without missing a beat, said that Taylor did it. He said he didn't, and the fight was on. "No, I didn't", "yes, you did", "no, I didn't", "yes, you did", all the way to the interstate. Then the cry from the back seat changed from "are we there yet?" to "how many minutes till we get there." Bonnie and I looked at each other with the same thought, a glass sound-proof barricade between the seats.

Traffic was pretty heavy as we turned off US-23 at Dundee and headed west on M-50. The last time the boys asked how many more minutes, we had gone from 75 minutes to 40, and they had finally settled in. A feud as to which one had their hand on whose side of the seat had developed and it was escalating. They reached the nuclear stage as we turned on US-12. The Irish Hill's go-cart track saved us from complete annihilation, as the boys recreated the wreck of the century from their last trip to the go-cart track. From what I could tell Zach was driving one cart, when Taylor in the second cart turned left in front of their mom in still another cart .... "How many minutes till we're there?" Talk about right turns, it's really difficult to remain in a conversation with grandkids and drive at the same time.

Why can't I roller blade in the Grand Canyon ?

KRD   21

W.J.Hayes State Park was just around the corner when the boys asked how many more minutes. The colors of fall were in full bloom as we passed the ranger station and headed towards the tall pines and campsite 131. We had camped there earlier in the spring, and number 131 is nestled between two sand ridges that are covered with old growth pine. Behind the ridge is a shallow swamp ringed with the red and gold of the late October maples.

Taylor and Zach in their Halloween costumes for 1995.

Why can't I roller blade in the Grand Canyon ?

KRD

We had no sooner pulled into the campsite when the doors of the Jeep popped open and the boys began the discovery process. The admonition "don't go near the swamp" was too late. Zach had fallen off a tree trunk that stretched itself across a narrow section of murky water which covered at least 28 inches of gooey muck. To this day I don't know how he managed to fall and only get his hands immersed in the muck. A quick trip to the water faucet, soap, and a paper towel, and he was back in business. Zach and Taylor continued where they had left off, I continued the unhooking process, and Bonnie was getting things ready to start dinner, when the unmistakable sound of soggy wet sneakers being pulled out of gooey mud was heard. Zach had made progress; he had gotten out at least five feet further into the swamp before he fell off the same log. This time he really did it! Grandma raised her voice, and even Taylor sought shelter. Taylor thought it was a real good idea to help me grill the pork chops. He figured that grandpa was a good buffer from the unleashed storm that was heading towards Zach and the gooey sneakers that extended up to his knees.

Dinner was a rather subdued affair, Taylor ate his potatoes without protest, and Zach asked for seconds on the green beans which he hates. They weren't sure just how long grandmas stay mad, so they were playing everything close to the vest. They even wanted to help with the dishes.

After the traditional campfire, it was an early night for the boys and we followed soon after.

I can't remember what I was dreaming about, but I had the vague feeling that someone was watching me. Light was just beginning to illuminate the curtains when I opened one eye, and Zach and Taylor were standing at the bedside looking at me. "Are you awake yet?" they asked in unison, "NO, and I won't be for another 30 minutes!" Zach picks up my arm, twists it so he can look at my watch, and says "we'll be back in 10 minutes." I said thirty, he said 10, we made it to 15 when they cheated. They turned on all the lights.

The two burner Coleman stove that we got as a wedding present in

Why can't I roller blade in the Grand Canyon ?

1967' came out of its hiding place and it wasn't long before the bacon pieces were sizzling in the cast iron skillet. Zach was busy mixing a dozen eggs in the Tupperware bowl, and when the bacon was just right the boys poured the eggs into the skillet. The sharp snap of bacon frying was replaced with the aroma of bacon and eggs mixing with the scent of fall in the crisp morning air.

With breakfast out of the way, the day's activities were already being planned out. Zach and Taylor were ready to follow the deer trails that we had discovered on our last visit. Before we left Toledo, Zach and I purchased enough plaster of paris to make casts of every deer in Michigan. I told them that they would have to remember where the trail began, and with just a little coaxing they were on the right track.

The fallen leaves covered the area between the lowlands, so it took them some time before they found useable prints. They cleared away the leaves and other debris, while I mixed the plaster of paris. Somehow Zach got plaster bits all over him, and Taylor was really interested in the salamander that crawled out of one of the plaster casts. We used what little water we had left to clean the plaster off the salamander, but he didn't look to good.

Boys can only wait so long for plaster casts to dry, so they quickly found another deer trail to an adjacent ridge. The pine covered ridge led us to another undiscovered .... campground area. If you listened to the boys talk as they skillfully guided us back to our campsite, they were the first people to enter the woods since the Indians. We arrived at the Airstream, or as the boys call it the silver bullet, just in time for lunch.

With our walk from the deer print area to the pine ridge and back to the campground we covered about 2 miles and the boys were fairly tired, well at least we were. Bonnie won the toss, and got lunch going, while I started to remove all the burrs that Zach and Taylor had managed to find. They thought it was all pretty neat, so we put all the removed burrs in an envelope so they could take them home and show mom. I wanted to put them in their coat pocket so they could show mom. With your own kids, revenge sometimes takes awhile.

Why can't I roller blade in the Grand Canyon ?

After lunch we had to go and check on the plaster casts, so we extended the hike over to the lake. The brisk wind was causing the waves to break across the sand beach and travel almost to the start of the picnic grounds. The Canadian geese had sought shelter in the parking lot, and we were the only people walking the beach. There used to be a trail which followed the lake and eventually wound its way to the top of a fairly large hill which overlooks the entire lake.

We found the trail, and eventually the overlook, but sections of the walk way had been replaced with stairs and blacktop. The ease in which we had made the climb diminished the exhilaration that we had experienced in earlier times with the view.

We decided to continue our journey to the seldom used side of the hill near the small boat channel to Round Lake. Zach and Taylor raced ahead and weaved their way between the boulders as they followed the narrow causeway into Wampler's Lake. We thought there might be a repeat of the tennis shoes in the swamp incident, but the boys managed to keep their footing. There were several fishermen coming in off the wind blown lake and you could tell from their wet clothes and drawn looks that they had not been successful.

The intermittent blue skies and sunshine were gradually replaced with ominous shades of gray, and when the sun did make a fleeting appearance, the clouds coming from the North Country darkened to the color of fresh concrete. We had brought pieces of oak with us from our last stay in southern Ohio, and it wasn't long before the oak had been transformed into the perfect fire for strip steaks. Through some quirk in their childhood development Zach and Taylor prefer hot dogs to steak, so they were given the hot dog fork. The temperature had been dropping steadily all day, and drizzly rain replaced the intermittent sun. By the time the steaks were finished the picnic table was out of the question, and the Airstream became a warm and friendly place to be. While Bonnie and I did the dishes, the boys found an interesting program on TV. It was either that or another marathon game of Monopoly. By 8:30 the adventurers were sound asleep, and Bonnie and I were in our night attire by 9.

Why can't I roller blade in the Grand Canyon ?

In the early morning, sometime between darkness and the first shades of red in the eastern sky, I again had the feeling that someone was watching me. "Grandpa, Grandpa, wake up". Taylor was whispering, "There's an eye that's been watching me". Somewhere between the whisper and recognition the adrenalin really kicked into high gear and I was looking for the "evil eye". Taylor had no trouble pointing it out, I needed my glasses. The life-saving brass button on my hat caught the reflected light in the trailer just right and it gave Taylor, with his kid's imagination, all the necessary ingredients for the "evil eye". The banishment of the hat to the dirty clothes hamper solved the problem.

With the "evil eye" exiled, Taylor had more important things to discuss, and the item with the highest priority was a toss up between: I'm hungry, and I've got to go to the bathroom. Bathroom won. With all the commotion in the trailer it wasn't long before the other worlds were stirring. The outside temperature had dropped to almost freezing, and frost covered everything. With a knowing glance in my direction Bonnie suggested McDonalds for breakfast, and getting dressed took on an added urgency for the boys. It must be really neat to get so excited by what we consider the simplest things.

With dumb luck on our part, we opted to head north when we left Wamplers' for the restaurant in Brooklyn. It was a good thing we made them eat first, because McDonalds' had just installed one of those gigantic indoor kids play area, and the boys were really excited. For the next hour an a half we only caught glimpses of them as they explored the maze of tunnels, spheres, and slides that were open to them. Bonnie and I concluded that McDonalds ought to give the food away and charge for the play area. We settled in and had another cup of coffee.

By the time we left McDonalds the day was beginning to show promise. The sun was gradually warming things up and the temperature was showing signs of life. When we pulled into the campground, Mother Nature and her box of crayons had been busy. The reds and yellows of the fallen leaves, enhanced with the green

Why can't I roller blade in the Grand Canyon ?

hues of the pines, really made the deep blue of the sky impressive.

After lunch we headed for the plaster casts with the boys new friend, Lindsay. Lindsay was from the next campsite and she sort of adopted Taylor. Zach is too cool for girls and besides he still thinks girls are "yuckey", except for mom and grandma of course. The funny part of this whole story is that Zach gave Lindsay one of the plaster prints so she could have one for "show and tell" at school, Taylor got all upset.

I thought that I had been very careful with my choice of adjectives, especially with the boys around. However, when I called the driver of a car that pulled out in front of us a "Butt Head", I knew that I had committed a mortal sin. Never use terms, especially those that sound neat, in front of Zach and Taylor. On the other hand, it was funny watching Bonnie trying to explain to the boys what a "butt head" is.

Renee was weeding the flower bed in the front yard as we pulled up, and couldn't wait to get a big hug and kiss from her family. Meanwhile, the boys were mapping out a strategy to avoid any such displays of public affection. They haven't learned that moms are a lot smarter than young boys. Renee was two steps ahead of them and successfully blocked every avenue of their planned escape. It wasn't long before she had both of them rounded up, and in her arms.

Our son Jeff and his son Trevor.

Why can't I roller blade in the Grand Canyon ?

Bonnie and I had planned a long fall color camping weekend at Three Lakes, one the Upper Peninsula's National Forest Campgrounds, with our good friends Doug and Sue Mefferd of Troy, Ohio. But, like a lot of things, our plans seem to be subject to last minute changes, and last weekend was no exception.

It's funny how one small change in the day's routine can have a profound effect on everything to follow. Wednesday night we got a call from Dan asking us to watch the boys before school Thursday morning. Sometime between being dropped off and leaving for school, Bonnie and I had promised to take them camping. So much for the U.P.

Flatulence, or farts, commonly brings giggles and grins from boys the age of Zach and Taylor, and speaking from experience, they are no exception. We couldn't have gone fifty feet before the trailer's torsion bars gave forth a mighty groan as the Jeep & trailer negotiated the first of many turns. The sound of metal rubbing against metal exactly matched the sound that emanates from Taylor's intestinal tract, and Zach was quick to divert the blame to his little brother. Taylor, who was quietly trying to figure out how to punch his brother without getting caught by Nana & Papa, forgot all about the equities of brawling in the back seat as he launched his counter measures. Zach was giggling so hard that he offered little resistance as the two of them fought for dominance from the safety of their seat belts.

For young boys, control of the back seat is especially tiring after a full day of school and "kill the teacher." By the time we reached Samaria Road the boys were sound asleep, and the groaning of the torsion bars went unnoticed.

Our favorite campsite was available and I had three experts relaying instructions and guiding my efforts at backing up the trailer. With three different opinions as to the "best" location, things were not going very well. Bonnie thought it would be a good idea to take the boys to the men's room. Earlier she had spotted the contortions that had overtaken Taylor, and Zach was already looking at several

Why Can't I Roller Blade in the Grand Canyon

trees that would meet his requirements. With a shrug of my shoulders came the realization that the boys were just doing their job. It was the first of many inspections they would carry out during the weekend.

When the boys got back, Zach got the hand crank for the jacks, and started to level out the trailer. I had showed him how to do that operation earlier and now he considered that his contribution to setting up camp. Taylor was busy exploring the campsite, and dragging back wood for the night's campfire.

Grandpa, Grandma, Taylor, with Zach behind the lense.

Why Can't I Roller Blade in the Grand Canyon

The boys and I made several trips into the woods to locate just the right type of dry wood for the evening's fire. They even helped to saw the oak limb into pieces that would fit into the fire ring. It wasn't long till the novelty had worn off the saw, and they weren't arguing as to whose turn it was. As I took the saw from their hands we talked about the "lumber jack dollars" that I was making for them, and right away Taylor wanted to know where he could spend them. Carefully, we counted the rings of the "dollar," and I showed them how the tree grew, and how to tell the good growth years from the bad. Zach became very quiet as he recounted the 28 growth rings, and then with a great deal of thought he said, "This tree is almost as old as Mom."

After dinner Taylor quickly laid claim to starting the campfire and with some expert advice from his brother, the paper, kindling, and bigger stuff were properly dumped into the fire pit. Taylor had a little difficulty with the safety matches, twelve of them to be exact. Finally he got one of the safety matches to light, and he carefully guarded the flame as he touched each corner of the exposed paper. The campfire came to life with a couple of well placed puffs, as the last rays of sun light filtered through the pines. Soon the lure of the campfire was replaced with the cold of the night, and "X-Files" at 9.

With popcorn and hot chocolate for the kids and "Tums" for myself, we settled into our respective places before the TV set. I'll have you know that we're roughing it, I had to manually change the channels on the black and white set, and I even had to set the temperature on the forced air furnace. The things that I have to put up with to camp in the wilderness.

We tried to watch their favorite show, the X-Files, which started at 9, but by 9:02 Taylor was already curled in a ball sound asleep. By the first commercial break Zach was imitating his brother. Bonnie had the fore sight to have the boys sleeping accommodations all ready, so all I had to do was pick them up and carry them to their waiting sleeping bags in the front of the trailer. Bonnie and I tried to watch the end of the program, but we were both drifting off by the next break. I still don't know how we did it when our kids were that age. Maybe we're just getting older.

The difficulty with getting up at 6:15 am for work is that after a while it becomes automatic. Nestled in the tall pines, and with the trailer's shades drawn, the first glimpses of light are confusing. I thought that I had seen Zach sit up in bed and it wasn't long before Taylor had joined him. With as much stealth as they could muster, they headed for our bed.

"What time is it," asked Zach. Without moving I replied, "Two in the morning, go back to bed." Quicker than quick, Zach grabbed my wrist illuminating the digital dial on my Timex. "It is not! It's 7:34." cried Zach. "Besides," said Taylor, "I have to go to the bathroom."

Remembering the hot chocolate and the cans of Squirt from the night before, it was only a matter of minutes before we were heading towards the modern two-holers. As the three of us walked along the path, Zach asked why they couldn't use the bathroom in the trailer. Thinking of several possible responses, I settled on the one that the boys wouldn't question. Looking them both straight in the eye I lied, "Because it's Nana's." I didn't dare tell them the real reason, something about their aim.

Breakfast was our usual scrambled eggs and bacon pieces all mixed together. Zach breaks the eggs and Taylor dumps in the bacon, while I managed the toaster. While the boys finished their breakfast watching the "Super Heros", Bonnie and I planned the morning activities. We decided that the threat of rain was not going to dampen our planned hike over to Wampler's Lake. The boys called the hike "going to the sun."

The rain caught up with us as we reached the skiing beach, near the small boat channel to Round Lake. By the time we huffed and puffed to the top of the overlook we had found; a red pen, a golf ball, a quarter, duck and goose tracks, and some excellent white tail deer prints. We even found Taylor's shoe that he managed to run right out of as the boys raced down the hill towards the swimming beach.

Why Can't I Roller Blade in the Grand Canyon

Breakfast at the campsite.

After lunch we took to the car and headed over towards Brooklyn, and the Pine Tree Antique Mall. As we entered the mall, the owner looking at the boys with apprehension, decided to ensure their good manners with a bribe. Taylor was easy, he took the first sucker that was offered, but Zach being older and wiser held out for grape.

The boys really enjoyed the tour through Michigan International Speedway, and were really impressed when I told them that Nana and Papa had driven the Corvette around the track. As we overlooked turn one on the 2.5 mile oval the boys really started asking questions. I'll admit I stretched the truth a little about our time on the track, but with Bonnie looking on, the "lies" were reduced to embellishments, and the boys said "yeah, right" only a couple of times.

The next stop on the afternoon tour of the "Irish Hills" was the Walker Stage Coach Stop. We walked the grounds of the first stage coach inn on the north side of U.S. 12, and then visited the "brick" Walker Tavern on the south side.

Walker Tavern, US 12 and Michigan route 50, Cambridge Junction.

Zach opened the front door for Bonnie as the wind pushed us into the foyer. With three rooms of antiques beckoning, and a stairway to explore, the boys were considering their options. Sensing their indecision I asked, "OK who's coming with me?" Without missing a beat they both announced in a unified loud voice, "We"re going with Nana." There were two ladies coming down the narrow tilted stairs that had over heard the conversation, and as they passed by in the narrow confines of the hall I could see the laughter that they had shared. The older of the two whispered to me "grandma's are always more fun," the younger one just smiled, but I knew they were right.

Campground Frisbee lost its appeal to the boys as they watched a small tree frog making its way across the road. Picking the frog up by it's rear leg got the desired result from one of their campground friends, as she screamed, "get that thing out of my face." Grandma was the next victim, and she played the part perfectly. The boys, extremely pleased with the results of their latest adventure, decided that the frog would be much happier in a plastic cup that had just a little Pepsi left in it till they decided what to do with it. Evidently when I told them to let him go back to his mommy and daddy they decided the frog would be more comfortable in the trailer. Later that night the frog managed to escape the confines of the 16 oz plastic cup, even though they had given him some Pepsi to drink.

You should have heard Bonnie when that frog landed on her face just after midnight. I still don't know how she sat up and turned on every light in the trailer, and still managed to keep the covers tight around her neck. When my eyes, shaded from the sudden light, started to focus I found the frog sitting on top of the television just looking at us. Evidently, when Bonnie sat up she must have launched the frog on a perfect trajectory towards the TV. And there the frog sat wondering what all the commotion was about.

After several attempts at capture, Zach and Taylor were finally successful, and the frog went out the door to join its family. When I finally got back to bed, Bonnie was still in the bathroom washing her face. Zach and Taylor were silently snickering about their latest coup, while they feigned sleep snug in their sleeping bags. We could just imagine the laughter lines beginning to form right below the chin line, adjacent to their dimples.

Sunday was great! Rocket Frog as the frog incident would later be called was in the past, and Grandma was even talking to the boys as she prepared breakfast. However, she was heard to ask the boys if they wanted frog legs for lunch.

God! We had a great time.

Three generations of the Dickson Family: Grandpa, Trevor, and Jeff.

It was Renee's weekend with the boys, and with an intended early Sunday morning departure it was decided that Zach and Taylor would spend Saturday night at 5630. When they arrived we were loading the trailer and their gear didn't slow us up a bit as everything was properly stowed in the silver bullet. With only the trailer left to hook up I asked Zach if he wanted his old job back. Leaping into action with Taylor at his side, he resumed the duties of last year's vacation. "Come on back Grandpa .... a little more

Why Can't I Roller Blade in the Grand Canyon

towards the house," exclaimed Zach, with Taylor a split second, later echoing the same instructions.

Watching from a distance Renee decided to relive one of the highlights of camping that delighted her and Jeff, and drove their father right up the wall. "Dad, your heading wrong! Your about a foot off to the left." With those instructions, and an immense smile spreading across her features, Renee became even more animated in her directions. Since I wasn't listening to them, Zach and Taylor returned to their game of drive way catch, and Renee doubled over with laughter, continued her dubious directions. With several missed attempts behind us, I decided to have a look for myself. As I headed towards the rear of the Jeep, Renee retreated to the safety of her mother. Bonnie, with a look of disgust that only she can give, says, "Renee are you picking on your father again?"

With the flatlands behind us, and Zach and Taylor firmly in control of the backseat, the Jeep's speedometer hovered around 58 as we sped down I-75 past the Grayling, Michigan, city limits. Using the Ninja Turtles and Superman to defend the left side of the seat, and Batman and the Land Shark to defend the integrity of the right, Zach and Taylor were hard pressed to call a cease fire when Grandma said, "Boys, look at the flock of wild turkeys."

Hiding right behind the "Welcome" sign were 26 wild turkeys, Zach says there were 28 and Taylor is waiting for the instant reply before he commits himself. It was difficult counting the number of turkeys and listening to Bonnie talk about dinner at the same time, but there were 26. After all, we had nothing planned for dinner, and after a tedious day of driving, roasted turkey would certainly be tasty.
....

I must have startled the turkeys when I swerved because they all went straight up as we knocked over the "Welcome to Graying" sign. As we passed under the turkeys, the windshield wipers were having a devil of a time removing the grit that accompanied their leavings. It was very difficult seeing where we going after that. I remember thinking that turkeys couldn't fly when Zach, our oldest

Why Can't I Roller Blade in the Grand Canyon

and wisest grandson, recalled from a science lesson that they could if they made themselves light enough.

With the windshield wipers on high and the squirters straining to keep up, I felt the momentum of the car change. Peering through the gray streaks that the wipers were leaving behind on the windshield, I found that the Jeep and Airstream had left the narrow confines of the Interstate, and were now hurtling down a rock strewn ravine, weaving between the cedars and white spruce in our path. I didn't even have time to turn off the wipers before we plunged into a roaring stream. I lost no time shifting into 4-wheel drive as we followed the rushing water down the twists and turns of the thinning water way of the south fork of the AuSable.

With all the white water cascading over the Jeep, the windshield finally cleared up and even from the confines of the backseat Zach and Taylor had no difficulty in seeing the waterfall. With only enough time to fasten our seatbelts we were soon heading south towards the very center of Crawford County. It's a good thing it was only a small drop because when we went under the water the trailer acted like a gigantic bobber and brought us right back to the surface. I shifted the jeep into 4-wheel drive low and managed to climb back to the interstate. As we left the roar of the waterfall behind I could hear Bonnie's voice coming through the piano melodies of Teddy Wilson.

KEN! **KEN!!**

Didn't you hear Zach and Taylor? They have to go to the bathroom. Stop at the next rest area, the boys have to use the bathroom. OK?

I was still wondering about the wild turkeys. What a day-dream.

I realized that we were pushing our luck when the twin ivory colored towers of the Mackinac Bridge appeared in the rear view mirror. The boys had been in the car for six hours, and Andrus Lake would be another hour and a half added to the total. Warfare broke out as we passed Moran. Both boys had their shoes off, and during the

Why Can't I Roller Blade in the Grand Canyon

scuffle for back seat supremacy, here after known as the "Sock Battle," Zach managed to push Taylor off the seat and into the foot well. At which point, Zach claiming his territorial right, lays down on the back seat, all the while proclaiming victory. Meanwhile, Taylor frantically searching for some sort of a secret weapon grabs his dirty smelly socks, and with one movement lands on top of his brother with the "SOCKS" a fraction of an inch from Zach's nose. Very calmly Taylor announces to Zach, "I've got SOCKS, and I'm not afraid to use them." At this point the mean old Grandma intervened, and I never did find out what he intended to do with the SOCKS. One can only guess. From this point on, the Dickson family annals will refer to this as the "Sock Maneuver."

Mackinac Bridge and Mackinac Lighthouse.

Eight hours later, two rain storms, and a heavy head wind the last 50 miles; we are back at Andrus Lake and some of the same old unnamed bug-a-boos have returned to haunt our good time with Zach and Taylor. If you remember from last years fall camping trip,

Why Can't I Roller Blade in the Grand Canyon

we left Andrus Lake just after supper, because I felt extremely uncomfortable with something. Can't tell you what it was ..... still don't have a clue. .... But when we pulled into the campground the same unnamed fears returned. This time we are not alone in the campground, so perhaps I'll start feeling better as I rationalize my irrational feelings. Bonnie just says I'm nuts. Perhaps.

Campsite at Andrus Lake, Upper Peninsula.

With Zach and Taylor's help, we located last year's campsite, and within minutes the trailer was unhooked and expertly leveled. The blue skies and sunshine hid the fact that the temperature hovered in the high fifties, and swimming was replaced with thoughts of long pants and jackets. As the boys bounced from the confines of the

Why Can't I Roller Blade in the Grand Canyon

trailer to the expanse of the surrounding pine forest they started exploring the southwest shore of the lake. The boys found the start of the fern covered trail that we used last year, and it wasn't long till they were rushing headlong into the forest. With the help of thousands of hungry mosquitoes our wood gathering expedition was of short duration as we hurriedly returned to the open spaces of our campsite.

With guidance from Papa, Zach and Taylor soon had a blazing campfire illuminating the gloom of the impending weather change that was occurring over Lake Superior. A nice bed of coals shortly replaced the towering flames, and it wasn't long before the hamburgers which were cooked to perfection joined the rest of the balanced meal on the picnic table. I was a little slow finishing my burger, and when I reached for my peaches, Zach and Taylor were polishing off my last bites.

The temperature dipped to a low of 38 degrees Sunday night, and the campfire lost its appeal as the sun disappeared behind a stubborn cloud bank brought in from the wind whipped Lake Superior. The catalytic heater had been in service almost all day, and as darkness approached with the chill of the north country, it made the trailer warm and secure. Zach wanted to watch TV, and Taylor was undecided as to the night's activities. Bonnie and I had decided earlier that the boys were going to write their parents every night describing the highlights of their day, and this was a good time to start.

With the day's activities thoughtfully reduced to several lines and carefully sealed away in envelopes for postal delivery, Zach and Taylor were ready for bed. The davenport of the Airstream makes into a double bed and with practiced effort the boys rolled out their sleeping bags and staked out their territory, as they quickly prepared for bed. Sleep came within seconds amidst charges of "we're not tired." The first muffled thump was about midnight, and in the dim light of our reading lamp, I could see Taylor huddled in a little ball, completely out of his sleeping bag, wedged under the shelf of the front window; and Zach, on the floor still clutching his pillow, with his legs stretched out across the bed. Within several moments I set their world aright, and sleep returned to our little corner of Andrus Lake.

Lower Falls of the Tahquamenon River.

I thought that Zach and Taylor were going to sleep all day, but the crisp sound of bacon frying in an iron skillet brought the boys to the screen door with the question; "Papa!, Are you going to put the bacon in with the scrambled eggs?" The cool brisk morning showed signs of promise as the boys finished off the last drops of tea from their metal camping cups. The boys had discovered a new source for stones, and they even succeeded in topping last years skipping record, when I handed Zach the folded wood saw and Taylor the coiled line that we would use to drag the wood back to the campfire. Remembering the hungry mosquitoes from last night, a liberal application of Avon's manly "Skin So Soft" was high on our list. Last night's chill was still lingering in the recesses of the deep pine as we detoured across a cut over section of the state forest. This would be the fifth season for the blueberries that had quickly taken over the clear cut, and from the budding present in the plants, the third week in August should be just about right. Ignoring Nana's warnings about pulling the leaves off small branches, Taylor was looking for sympathy, while trying to hold back the tears, as the blood flowed from the jagged cut on his finger. By this time we were about a ten minute walk from camp, and after a quick consultation Zach and I decided to follow the two track deeper into the clear cut, while Nana and Taylor returned for Neosporin and a band aid.

Zach was the first to hear the distinctive sound of the Sand Hill cranes, and it wasn't long before the field glasses found their location as they foraged in the tall ferns. With a little help, Zach found the Crane's tracks indicating where they had crossed the loose sand, and with the wind in our favor, we tried to get closer for a better look. Quietly covering the distance that separated our quarry, our steps mindful of the brittle debris left behind by the loggers, a deep growl from a red Jeep in four wheel drive low caught the bird's attention, and sent them to flight. Momentarily disappointed, we were glad to see them when we realized just how far we had tracked the cranes across the clear cut. The drive back to camp had Zach describing in minute detail how we followed the birds across the clear cut, and at the same time, Taylor was describing all the gory details of his cut finger.

We spent the greater part of the afternoon counting the steps to the Upper and Lower Falls of the Tahquamenon, and while Taylor doesn't believe that the Tahquamenon River is the source for root beer anymore, Zach almost had him convinced to taste the water just to make sure. The rowboats to the Lower Falls drew the boys like magnets as they raced down the path to the boat landing. As Bonnie paid the attendant the required six dollar rental fee, the boys were already fastening their life jackets, and expressing in magnificent detail to anyone that would listen how they canoed the Manistee River with their Dad. With all the confidence an eight year old can muster, Zach directed Bonnie and I to the bow and stern seats, Taylor to the port oar, and Zach took his place at the starboard oar. The attendant gave us a mighty shove, the boys placed the oars in the water, and the sluggish current did most of

Why Can't I Roller Blade in the Grand Canyon

the work on our "three hour tour." Perhaps we'll do better next year.

Just a few of the finer rowing points, Zach & Grandpa.

The road to Vermillion Life Saving Station parallels Lake Superior about a mile inland on an ancient sand ridge through the second growth pines and hemlock of the state forest. In the past, about an hour before sunset, we have found deer grazing on the grasses along the sides of the dirt road, and with the boys glued to the Jeep's windows we headed out past Shelldrake Dam. We didn't see even one deer along the way, but with the binoculars trained into the passing forest Taylor saw a bear. On the other hand, Zach said Taylor was looking through the field glasses backwards and it was really a bug on the window.

Why Can't I Roller Blade in the Grand Canyon

With the days dishes washed and put away, the firewood that we had gathered, would now have to be cut to length and split to feed the evenings campfire. Zach and Taylor were arguing over whose turn it was, and who was going to go first, as they brought the saw and hatchet to the make shift saw horse. The enthusiasm that accompanied them to the wood pile dissipated with the initial strokes of the saw, and it wasn't long before Zach and Taylor were plotting their escape.

The reflection of the full moon slowly worked its way across the lake to illuminate our corner of Andrus Lake. Marshmallows and a expertly whittled spruce branch, a sweatshirt and a comfortable chair placed close to the wood fire, were the boy's companions, as the brilliant reds of the sunset surrendered their glow to the campfire's embers. Sleep came softly Monday night.

Bonnie and I awoke to the sunrise call of the loons as their signature echoed across the still waters of the lake. Dressing quietly, it wasn't long before the aroma of fresh brewed coffee enticed Bonnie to join me at the waters edge. Several fishermen were already casting their best lures into the lake's weed bed in a practiced effort to entice the bass to join them for breakfast. Others were trying for the pike that rose from the deep troughs to feed in the shallows that surrounded the lake. While we watched from the canopy of the pine forest, life slowly returned to the state forest camp ground.

I had started the bacon frying on a low heat, and was scrambling the eggs, when Bonnie joined me at the picnic table. Pouring her a second cup of coffee, she looked at me and said, "The boys told me that they aren't getting up, and that you can't make them." Zach and Taylor must have been listening because my, "What did they say?" was greeted with laughter intermixed with giggles. "Come on boys, lets get dressed," was acknowledged with, "You can't make us!" and more whispered giggles. As I entered the trailer, heads retreated to the safety of their sleeping bags, and hands tightly closed the openings behind them. Threats and carefully aimed

Why Can't I Roller Blade in the Grand Canyon

pokes only brought more muffled laughter from the boys. So without further delay I picked up each bag and shook, eventually each of the boys rolled out and onto the floor. The early morning wrestling match was underway.

The retired couple in the next campsite had an old dented aluminum fishing boat tied to a tree on the bank that just intrigued Zach and Taylor, and each morning they would go over and check it out. This morning Mr. Bateski must have been waiting for them, because they raced back with the fishing poles that he had set up for their use. Bonnie and I walked over and introduced ourselves, and in the discussion that followed the boys managed to get a dozen night-crawlers. Within minutes Mr. and Mrs. Bateski were heading across the lake, and I was trying to figure out how to get Zach's line off the pine branch that had gotten in the way of his perfect cast. Taylor soon lost interest, especially after Zach's second cast landed a strike. And that's the way the morning unfolded. The final tally was thirteen small perch and several large-mouth bass. Not bad from a lake that Doug and I have fished for years with no luck, and Zach wouldn't let either of us forget it either. That night Zach wrote Uncle Doug a letter with only one line ...... "Uncle Doug, I caught 13 more fish in this lake than you and Papa ever did."

The boys kept hoping for warmer weather to go along with the sunshine so we packed up and headed for Brimley State Park at the bottom of Whitefish Bay. Brimley had experienced an early morning thunderstorm that had been preceded by two days of steady rain, and most of the campers were drying out or had left as we arrived. With our choice of campsites awaiting our decision, we located a great campsite behind the dunes, and it wasn't long before Zach and Taylor had discovered the beach. Lunch was followed with swimsuits and promises not to go in the water for an hour as they raced down the path to the beach.

The rain clouds which had been a frequent visitor in the last couple of days were being pushed out of the area by the winds sweeping across Lake Superior from north of Wawa, and the waves pounding the shoreline were greeted with delight. Zach and Taylor raced each wave into the lake and then raced back to shore again. Some they won, but most they lost. While technically they had not gone into the water, the jury would not have taken long to convict, as the wet swimsuits gave them away. The waves were probably two to three feet, and while running away from one that Zach jumped over, Taylor lost his balance, and the wave crashed over him. With his pride severely damaged, Taylor decided to join us on the beach. Wrapping himself from head to toe in a beach towel Taylor was content watching Zach body surf the incoming waves.

Body surfing in Lake Superior at Brimley State Park.

With our new campsite came electricity and the boys were in for a real backwoods treat. As they surfed through all eighty channels on the television, Zach was disappointed that there was only one

Why Can't I Roller Blade in the Grand Canyon

station that he could get to come in, and try as hard as he could he just couldn't get the color to come in on the black and white set. The boys are big baseball fans, Nana made popcorn, and the fact that the commentary was in French was not going to deter their "big" evening. During one exciting play I asked Zach what the sportscaster had just said. Without taking his eyes off the unfolding play, Zach said, "Hit the damn ball, that's what you're getting paid for!" Bonnie and I just started laughing. I guess there are certain phrases that are universal in every language.

Even though the boys were writing their parents every night, they were really looking forward to talking to them Thursday night. We walked to the phone which was at the ranger station and waited for our turn on the phone. After the call to their parents, I placed a call to our son Jeff, and the boys waited like gentlemen on the park bench. Well almost, even the biker couple on the big Harley could hold their interest only so long. Within minutes "Big Time Wrestling, WWF Style" had broken out. The lady had remained on the bike while her husband went to register, and she was taking an avid interest in the boy's activities. Myself, I told them to quit acting like their mother, and to cut it out. Zach and Taylor both looked at me, and I could tell what was running through their heads, "He's over there on the phone, and we're over here." With three giant steps I caught up with Zach and swung him up on my shoulder. Taylor decided to come to the aid of his brother and leaped from the park bench towards his brother's tormentor. I caught him in mid-flight, and swung him up on the other shoulder. By this time the couple on the Harley was laughing so hard that they had both dropped their helmets. I really surprised myself, the boys had gained a lot of weight since the last time I tried that stunt. Later that night I was glad Bonnie had packed the BenGay.

We had a great time.

P.S. Every incident described in this narrative really happened. If you don't believe me, ask Zach & Taylor.

Why Can't I Roller Blade in the Grand Canyon

This coming week Zach and Taylor are planning our camping trip into the wilds of the Upper Peninsula. We should have their company for about ten days or so and hopefully we'll make the Porcupine Mountains near Ashland, Wisconsin, and Copper Harbor, Michigan.

At this point, I should mention that Taylor is not completely satisfied with the proposed excursion. It seems that Taylor wanted to include the Rocky Mountains on the proposed itinerary. From his highly educated second grade perspective, mountains are mountains, and if Zach gets the Porkies he should get the Rockies. When the older brother gets his way, logic and reason book no truths with an eight year old, and Taylor, while listening to my explanation, didn't believe a word of it.

Reading the disappointment in his eyes, I tried another tact. "Taylor, do you remember traveling to Andrus Lake last year, and how long it took?" Looking at his brother Zach for help, and sensing none forth coming, Taylor begrudgingly nodded his head. Noticing the change in Taylor's concentration, I continued. "The Porkies are going to take two long days traveling in the car, and to travel to the Rocky Mountains would take four long days. Maybe we can go next year." Taylor turned around and gave Zach a superior look of triumph. The only part of the whole conversation that registered with Taylor was the fact that next year we would go where he wanted to go.

Depending upon your historical perspective, the preparations for Operation's Overlord and Desert Storm, paled in comparison with Zach and Taylor's combined planning for their mid-summer assault on Michigan's Porcupine Mountains. Several weeks ago, Bonnie and I stopped at the Michigan Welcome Center on I-75, and gathered an arm full of brochures describing in vivid Kodachrome vignettes, the scenic wonders of the Upper Peninsula. The wonders of the brilliant multi-colored sunrise over Porcupine Mountain's Lake of the Clouds, and the utter darkness of the Delaware Copper Mine in the Keweenaw held the boys as the pamphlet's magic worked another illusion. The subdued hues of the Northern Lights reflecting off Lake Superior, held the boys enthralled as they worked their way through an advertiser's delight.

It took the boys several weeks, numerous phone calls, and two packs of notebook paper, to arrive at what they considered a schedule worthy of their time and endeavor. The Airstream or silver bullet will travel along the fabled sandy shores of Lake Michigan to the jack pine covered Porcupine Mountains. Along the much traveled route 41, we'll pass through Fort Wilkins and hike to the Estivant Pines, and perhaps the boys will discover the hidden truth of Lake Fanny Hooe. Munising, and Pictured Rocks, beckoned the boys with their much touted glass bottomed boat tour of the historical shipwreck coast line, and let's not forget the walking tour of Grand Island with the haunted lighthouse, to round out the whirlwind trek through the Upper Peninsula.

Bonnie and I had eagerly awaited Zach and Taylor's arrival Sunday night, but with last minute rides and brilliant fireworks, their departure time from Cedar Point was consequently delayed. Dan dropped the boys off about 12:30, and by the time we got their gear stowed, it was probably close to one before we got to bed. The much scheduled 5 a.m. departure from 5630 for the fabled North Country failed to materialize, as visions of Sunday's excursion to the Point filled the boy's dreams.

With barely enough light to properly survey the topography of the back seat, Zach and Taylor equally sub-divided the area and literally staked out their real estate. To properly guard against unwarranted trespass, the boys stationed action figures Batman, Robin, Superman, and Hulk Hogan at strategic locations. I'm not quite sure how the alarm system was activated, because within minutes after our departure, the boys were sound asleep.

Zach and Taylor woke up a little south of the Zilwaukee Bridge, and their secret back seat discussions centered on certain aspects of the trip north. After much deliberation, they settled on three demands: McDonalds for breakfast, somores around the campfire, and bacon fixed in with the scrambled eggs. The appearance of

Why Can't I Roller Blade in the Grand Canyon

the "Golden Arches" at the next exit quickly settled the first. The other requests were hammered out during the second round of bacon-egg-cheese biscuits.

One of Zach's new responsibilities was to touch each of the trailer's hubs for excessive heat, and after accomplishing the task during our lunch stop, he asked why the trailer was dripping. A quick check of the interior led to the shower compartment where one of the two five gallon water drinking water jugs had split a seam, and had inundated the rear of the trailer. While our flood didn't compare with the Biblical account in Genesis, there were to be far reaching ramifications for the inhabitants of the Silver Bullet. The second water jug, while intact, had joined its companion and rolled around in the flooded shower compartment, and we both agreed that since the toilet occupied the common space ..... well you get the picture.

Three hundred sixty two miles and seven hours after we started our journey, we arrived at Brevort Lake National Forest campground, for the first stay of our journey. Within minutes Zach and Taylor had found the hidden trail to the beach, tested the water, skipped rocks, and each had gotten a "soaker." With Zach leading the return to the trailer, the boys jumped from stump to stump, carefully avoiding the poison ivy patches which paralleled the forest path. It was during the last leap, that Zach was able to find the only pile of dog leavings in the entire campsite. Cleaning his soiled shoes on a part of unused shore line, Zach was heard to tell Taylor, "that wasn't dog stuff, it was BEAR."

With the frigid waters of Brevort Lake beckoning, the boys quickly changed to their swim trunks, and headed for the beach. The mid-eighties of the surrounding pine forest were replaced with the frigid waters of the lake, and the boys lasted about ten minutes. It's at this point in the narrative that if you ask the boys why they got out of the water so soon, they would tell the tale of the huge black water snake that attacked Taylor. Poppa would tell you the tale of an old stick lying on the sand bottom, magnified by the ripples on the lake that looked like a snake.

Why Can't I Roller Blade in the Grand Canyon

Leaving the brisk waters of Brevort Lake for the snuggling warmth of a beach towel, the boys quickly changed, and joined Bonnie and I at the campfire. The evening dishes were soon washed and returned to their proper niche, and it wasn't long before Zach returned with his unloaded camera and film. Despite the instructions and hands on experience that were forth coming from Taylor, we couldn't get the film to advance. So while Bonnie and Zach went to the pay phone to call Renee for proper instructions, Taylor and I sat around the campfire and talked about many things. We fed the glowing embers a variety of scrap wood from the workshop, and it wasn't long before the conversation turned to the world of a seven year old. With an extremely concerned look on his face, I could tell he was framing the question with all the seriousness he could muster. "Poppa, do you think the fire is ready for marsh-mallows yet?"

Taylor on the left and Zach on the right, caught in "Da Yooper's Tourist Trap."

Why Can't I Roller Blade in the Grand Canyon

An eminent philosopher once said, that a journey of 263 miles must start with a single step, but according to Taylor, it starts when Poppa attempts to hook up the trailer. Zach and Taylor must have taken lessons from their mother and Uncle Jeff, because two inches to the left ends up being six inches to the right, and the ball is never under the receiver. And then the laughter really starts.

From Brevort to the Porkies is 263 miles of narrow winding roads that are always on the incline, and the stretch of highway from the turn of the century ore docks, located on Marquette's waterfront, to the Yooper's Tourist Trap, west of Ishpeming, is an Airstreamer's nightmare. Twenty-eight miles of passing lane on a 48 degree incline, and two tanks of gas later, we arrived face to face with "Big Gus.'

"Big Gus" and Taylor and Zach at the "Yooper's Tourist Trap."

"Big Gus," was billed as the world's largest chain saw, and the cutting bar looked to be 23 feet long, as the "silver bullet" made its way into the parking lot. Zach had never seen a chain saw powered

Why Can't I Roller Blade in the Grand Canyon

by a full-blown 350 Chevy before, and Taylor was intrigued with the highly touted fifty-six Upper Peninsula outhouses on display, so the boys convinced Bonnie that the stop would be educational. Myself, well I couldn't believe that the whole thing was actually called a tourist trap, but then again. We left with two polished "leaver-rites," and a genuine piece of U.P. copper, that upon reflection looked a lot like a smashed penny. However, we all agreed that the two-holer outhouse, in the duplex style was well worth the visit.

Zach and Taylor pondering the possibilities of a duplex outhouse.

Tuesday's lunch stop was located just past the Mt.Shasta cafe,

Why Can't I Roller Blade in the Grand Canyon

between the town of Michigamme and Beaufort Lake. Incidentally, the cafe was used by Count Basie in the 1958 movie thriller "Anatomy of A Murder." The lunch was stacked ham sandwiches, on lightly toasted fresh baked wheat bread. We celebrated our good fortune with a vintage 1998 Pepsi, served chilled.

The Porkies welcomed our return with some of the meanest black flies that we have ever encountered. We retaliated with a Canadian tradition since 1951, Col. C. Coll's "Original Muskol." The result was a relatively bug free afternoon, except for Zach, the flies really liked Zach's knees.

Taylor and Zach at the entrance to the Porcupine Mountains.

Lake Superior determines the weather over the Porkies, and late Tuesday afternoon was no exception. The ominous storm clouds had started accumulating over the westerly Porcupine Mountain's Presque Isle campground, and arrived over Union Bay just past dinner. The first winds blew the Ivory suds and dirty dishes off the picnic table, and the second gust of frigid winds, blew the ashes from the fire pit over the members of the Dickson expedition. Abandoning the dirty dishes to the elements, we struggled to hold down the wild swings of the trailer's awning. It was quite a tussle, securing the awning, but the surging rain gusts aided our efforts. Taylor gathered the day's accumulation of dirty dishes from the ground, I finished washing the dishes, and Zach continued drying them. What a day!

We were soaked, and the evening's naturalist program was only minutes away. A hurried change of clothes, and a half mile walk through the pines to the Visitor Center, enabled us to avoid the last of the wind driven rain drops. The evening's program was a multi-media slide presentation of the four season recreational possibilities of the Porcupine Mountains. The 45 minutes were filled with a nocturnal glimpse of foxfire, the multi-colored hues of the Northern Lights, and of course the brilliant sunrises and captivating Lake Superior sunsets. The accompanying strains of Bach, Beethoven, Brahm, and Mozart, enhanced by the Bose surround sound system, completed the evening. The boys enjoyed the first five minutes, and after that they were sound asleep.

Union Bay Campground is within minutes of Central Standard Time, consequently darkness rarely arrives till almost 11. Refreshed from their 40 minute nap, the boys eagerly awaited the next stop on the itinerary. Passing the turnoff for the camp ground, and fortified with single dips of cookies and cream, the Dickson Expedition continued its westerly climb on Michigan route 107. The winding switchbacks deposited the Jeep Cherokee's inhabitants in a deserted parking lot, on the summit of a prehistoric Lake Superior beach line. A short walk through the stunted birch and aspen trees brought us to the granite escarpment framing the Lake of The Clouds. Wisps of fog hung in the valley, as the sounds of back packers hiking their way along the pine forested Carp River, worked their way to our vantage point. The gathering darkness in the east framed Government Peak, and highlighted the deep blue of Lake Superior. Zach was clearly taken with the stark beauty of a lone pine, blackened against the reddish hues of a spectacular Porcupine Mountain sunset. It was almost like saying grace, as

Why Can't I Roller Blade in the Grand Canyon

Zach said, "Cool," and Taylor, well he wanted to watch as he threw his cup of water over the precipice.

Taylor, Grandpa, and Zach at Lake of the Clouds, Porcupine Mountains.

Winter comes early, and stays late in the Porkies, and as we drove the twenty-four miles along the South Boundary Road, nature's spring bounty of wild-flowers was still evident. Our first planned stop was the Summit Peak hiking trail, twelve point two miles from

Why Can't I Roller Blade in the Grand Canyon

Union Bay camp ground. As we headed for the much used trail head, and recalling the gravel turn-off of many years ago, the asphalt picnic area came as quite a shock. The wooden out-houses have been replaced with a modern environmentally friendly comfort station. The rugged and manly switch-backs that tested our endurance in 1969, had been replaced with asphalt pathways and pressure treated stairs that lead the way through the forest to a 58' observation tower, on the peak of Summit Mountain. In some respects, Bonnie and I were great full for the improvements, but on another level, we wanted the boys to share our sense of exhilaration as we reached the peak and gazed upon Mirror Lake some thirty years ago. Things change over the years, but memories have a habit of improving.

Summit of Government Peak.

Why Can't I Roller Blade in the Grand Canyon

Continuing on the road to Presque Isle, on the western park boundary, the boys started to ask about our plans for lunch. It was only a half mile walk to Presque Isle river's Manido Falls, and we were prepared for two hungry boys. Zach had brought his napsack, and before we left the parking lot, we filled every nook and cranny with sandwiches, chips, snacks, and Pepsi. We had the much trodden path to ourselves, as we entered the flower filled meadow adjacent to the parking lot. Earlier, we had expressed the importance of silence on the boys, and as the boys raced ahead, Taylor suddenly stopped. Motioning for us, Taylor had spotted a fawn and four deer, and was pointing them out to Zach as we approached. The deer were munching their way through the ripening raspberries, parallel to a deeply wooden ravine, completely unaware of our presence. Our intrusion into their world continued for another five minutes. We were only twenty feet apart, when the winding mechanism on Zach's camera alerted them, and set them to flight.

After our experience with the deer, Manabezho Falls on the lower part of the river, didn't have the same holding power over the boys. However, the suspension bridge to the island, at the mouth of the river, brought the boys back to life, as they tested the engineer's design capabilities. First the bridge bounced up and down, and then much to their delight, they discovered they could make it pitch and yawl. The other passengers on the flight to the mainland were not overly impressed.

They slept most of the way back to the campground, and when they awoke it was with visions of swimming bouncing through their refreshed minds. The mid-eighty degree temperature brought only the campers to the sand beaches, and the sparkling waters of Lake Superior, and we were no exception. The boys swam, played in the surf, and held championship rock throwing contests till almost dinner, and protested vehemently when the umpire called time.

Zach and Taylor didn't display the same enthusiasm for the nature program on bats, as they did for the ice cream cones at a shop called "End of the Rainbow." Environmental practices have closed many of the Michigan black bear's preferred eating establishments, and the owners of the ice cream shop have had to improvise. They have discovered that discarded ice cream containers, coupled with an open dumpster full of delights, are must stops on the bear's daily rovings. Not only did the boys get their choice of flavors, but they were able to safely watch the antics of Yogi Bear, and two of his forest companions from the Jeep's backseat.

Zach & Taylor at Porcupine Mountain's Presque Isle.

Wednesday night the boys telephoned Mom and Dad, and Taylor was overheard to say that he wasn't having any fun. Bonnie and I had discussed this very possibility, and we were determined to enrich Taylor's part of the world. On the next leg of the journey, we decided to quiz Taylor on what he thought would be fun. With careful wording on our part, we engineered the conversation around to Taylor.

A brown bear at the Rainbow with his nose into a five gallon tub of ice cream.

"Taylor are you having fun yet?" Bonnie asked. With his eyes cast down Taylor replied, "No." I countered with, "Why not?" With his eyes twinkling, he replied "Because I don't have a girl friend." Zach sensing an opportunity to get even with his brother for some forgotten infraction said "Ask   him about Addy." "Wasn't Addy your girl friend?" Taylor, with a grin that grew larger as he spoke, said "Yeah, but she dumped me." Sensing an opportunity to help with Taylor's current difficulty, I asked if he wanted to send Addy a postcard from the Porcupine Mountains? "No, I'll find another one," replied Taylor as the gong sounded for the start of Round Two in the highly acclaimed B. W. F. (Backseat Wrestling Federation for those of you that have forgotten.) Sometimes you're just not prepared for the answers that can be forth coming from a seven

Why Can't I Roller Blade in the Grand Canyon

year old.

One hundred and thirteen miles after we left Union Bay, the birch tree lined canopy of U. S. Route 41 highlighted the last ten miles of our journey into Copper Harbor, and trek's end, Fort Wilkins. We had forgotten just how good the tone from the bell on the navigation buoy, guarding the harbor's entrance sounded. As Bonnie completed the camp site registration, the bell's tone kept repeating "welcome back Dickson's, welcome back." Our campsite was adjacent to the shores of Lake Fanny Hooe, and while we maneuvered the silver bullet, the boys renewed their rock throwing contest.

Fort Wilkins at the tip of the Keweenaw Peninsula.

With lunch out of the way, the boys discovered a spruce lined path along the rock strewn lake shore. With several hints from previous hikers, we followed the shore line to the gates of Fort Wilkins. There were several families enjoying the hospitality of the era, by assuming the dress and customs of the Fort. Several of the younger boys, dressed in cotton checked shirts and course weave pants, Suspenders, rope belts, and straw hats rounded out their period dress. They asked Zach and Taylor if they would like to try a toy they were playing with. It resembled a cup on a stick with a ball attached to the handle by a length of twine. The object was to get the ball into the cup. Zach being the oldest went first, and had no success, but Taylor landed a direct score on the first try. The boys, with their new companions, were off to explore the wonders of army life in the late 1800's.

Entrance to Fort Wilkins and the Copper Harbor campground.

Leaving the fort, we followed Fanny Hooe Creek through the towering pines, to the pebbled beach of Copper Harbor. On the west side of the mouth of the creek, stood an old weather beaten shingled house, with what appeared to be a cupola on the north end of the high peaked roof. Zach indicated to Taylor, the shape looked like a homing pigeon roost. Hearing the conversation, I pointed out to the boys that this was one part of an early Coast

Guard range light system, and in the window opening would have been a brilliant red light. Walking to the beach, and lining up the cupola with the harbor's entrance buoy we were able to locate the early range light's counterpart on the hill behind the house.

After dinner we decided to watch the sunset from the granite walled Copper Harbor overlook from the Brockway Mountain Drive. Our drive to the summit was not without the boys own brand of special entertainment. There soon came from the back seat voices from the Simpson's television program. "Miss Hoover, Miss Hoover!" came Taylor's best imitation of Ralph Wiggums, the police chief's son. "I ate my red crayon." Not to be out done, Zach answered with: "Miss Hoover, Miss Hoover! I glued my head to my shoulder." And Taylor replied with, "Miss Hoover, I ate my paste."

Chuckling at the boys faked soprano and their excellent rendition of "Ralph Wiggims," it suddenly dawned on us, that Zach and Taylor were imitating the whining little young lady in the adjacent campsite at Fort Wilkins.

The next twelve miles were variations on the same theme, and by the time Brockway Mountain Drive and route 26 merged on the outskirts of Eagle Harbor, Bonnie and I were ready for a change of traveling companions. Our salvation came in the form of a aged bent wood sign post indicating the location of Northwind Books. We had met the proprietors, Mr. & Mrs. VanPelt, on a previous trip to Eagle Harbor when their interesting shop was located in the Chief Warrant Officer's house, adjacent to the lighthouse. The Keweenaw Historical Society which operates the Eagle Harbor lighthouse as a nautical museum, needed additional space for artifacts from the MESQUITE, and the CITY OF BANGOR, and asked the VanPelt's to find other accommodations. Their new shop is located near the docks for the Harbor of Refuge, on the east end of the bay's narrow inlet. With Bonnie and I renewing old acquaintances, Zach and Taylor headed for the spacious front porch of the nineteen twenties stucco cottage. The well-worn leather and wicker furniture, lent itself to the comforts of coloring books, checkers, and time-honored children's books as the boys settled in for a comfortable stay. And if you visit the Northwind Book shop in the near future, you'll find two new pieces of early-vacation period art on the cottages knotty-pined front wall.

Before we leave the Keweenaw, I've got to mention the exploration of the Delaware Copper Mine by the Woods Expedition. Given his choice of activities, Bonnie and I thought that Zach would opt for the three mile trek through the pine covered two-tracks to the Estivant Pines, but alas the forty-five minute underground tour of a defunct copper mine really held his interest. With the first tour leaving at 10:00 A.M., Zach and Taylor made sure that we were first in line. As we donned bright yellow hard hats, and checked the Energizers in our official mine explorer flash-lights, the "Gilligan's Island" theme kept running through my head, "....... left for a three hour tour......" Earlier, I had expressed my dislike of closed in spaces, and Zach and Taylor remembering my hurried exit from the submarine COD, just said "Oh Poppa."

Modern miners at the Delaware Copper Mine.

Why Can't I Roller Blade in the Grand Canyon

The Keweenaw's early morning rise in temperature was being replaced with the cool damp air flooding from the mine as we descended the one hundred and twenty wooden stairs to the mine's first level. Evidence of decay and neglect were everywhere, and the safety railing with its loose wobble, did not inspire confidence in this apprehensive speleologist. The rusting mining tools left leaning against the tunnel's jagged out-croppings were conclusive evidence in my mind, that the miners dropped them when they made a hurried departure. The other visitors to this strange world saw the dilapidated tools as nothing more than turn of the century mining implements.

As the group made its way along the easterly drift, the guide pointed out the exhaustive safety features that were built into our tour. I only saw the electrical wires and 60 watt bulbs that illuminated the "Cheez-its" that I had dropped to blaze the trail to sunshine and warmth. The vein of copper, and the early miner's fortunes, ended an agonizing 900 feet, or 315 measured foot steps later with total darkness. According to the teenage guide, not being able to see your hand in front of your face is a cool thing. Zach and Taylor both agreed, myself, I had my fourth anxiety attack.

The early morning drive down the tree lined shore line of the Keweenaw Peninsula to the twin cities of Houghton Hancock brought us into the stark barren landscape of 19th century copper mines rusting in the morning sun. As the galvanized sheet metal skip towers and the natural rock steam power plant buildings lie in unwanted decay, the mines bare silent testimony to the regions prosperous past. When Bonnie and I pointed out the Portage Canal separating the cities, the boys were more interested in the on-going power struggle between good and evil that was taking place behind our seats.

The 187 miles from Fort Wilkins to Munising's Bay Furnace National Forest campground, was mostly downhill as we followed U.S. 41 past "DaYooper's Tourist Trap" to Marquette, and then Michigan's route 28 to Bay Furnace. The boys remembered all the important stops along the way, and the historical significance of each. They recalled "Big Gus," the outhouse collection, and the location of all the rest stops along the way. My concept of importance and theirs were on two separate tracks.

Zach was given the monumental decision of deciding what major Munising tourist attraction was going to get our money. We spent the better part of Saturday afternoon gathering the pertinent information on each of the three finalists. We capped the search before dinner, and compared notes during the evening's meal. Desert, and a decision, came with a celebration of double fudge sundaes at the Dairy Queen along Munising's lake front drive.

All the significant details were factored into Zach's conclusion: length of tour, what would be the attractions of the tour, and finally way down the list, my personal favorite ......cost. Zach and Taylor conducted interviews of previous tour participants (the campers on each side of us), compared the results with the claims of the brochures, and the outcomes were carefully evaluated. The Pictured Rocks Boat Tour at $66.00 came in second, and my personal favorite, the Grand Island Guided Tour at $48.00 came in a distant last. The Glass Bottomed Boat Shipwreck Tour, at $57.00 was the absolute, hands down winner. I asked the boys to re-evaluate their decision, but I knew that the island tour couldn't compete with visions of shipwrecks, and ghostly manifestations being revealed through "Miss Munising's" glass bottom.

The intact white oak planked canaler BERMUDA was a scant six feet below the surface of Grand Island's Murry Bay as the captain maneuvered "Miss Munising's" viewing panels expertly from bow to stern. An added bonus was a wooden staved barrel from the Williams Company, recently located and placed on the algae covered deck. Taylor was much more interested in the glass Budweiser bottle littering the stern deck that a recent visitor had left. The captain's white porcelain bathtub from the HERMAN METTLER was easily spotted a short distance away from the boilers and propulsion machinery. A trail of black iron ore from her disintegrating cargo hold led from the reefs edge to the remaining tamarack beam which formed her massive keel. Resting at right angles to the keel, were the remains of the port and starboard bow sections with their still closed port holes. Finishing the tour were the "bones" of the lumber hooker GROH. Her cargo of rough sawn white pine boards was quickly salvaged by the local inhabitants and according to "Miss Munising's" captain, provided quite a building boom to the community. Asked for Zach and Taylor's comments following the completion of the tour, they were heard to remark, "cool."

The Woods' Expedition to Lake Superior Shipwrecks.

Why Can't I Roller Blade in the Grand Canyon

After the lengthy fresh water voyage, a hurried trip to the post office, to post Saturday's mail to Mom and Dad, a quick stop at the hardware for Coleman fuel and we were on our way to Bay Furnace and dinner. Chicken and rice was the "entree of choice" at the Silver Bullet cafe, and Sunday night's repast proved to be without doubt one of the best. The banquet included beets, cottage cheese, crushed pineapple, and somores for dessert.

The time after dinner has fallen into a regular routine. I wash the days dishes, the boys write their Mom and Dad with a synopsis of the day's activities, while Bonnie drys. With the day's letters written, and posted, we were once again prepared to explore the wilds of the western end of Pictured Rocks National Lakeshore. A one point two mile hike, through the turn of the century burned over pine forest, brought us to the hardwood covered ridge which encompassed Miner's Falls. The Park Service has constructed a stairway to take visitors about half-way down the sandstone faced precipice adjacent to the falls for better viewing, and Zach and Taylor appreciated their efforts.

According to the castle experts that we had with us, the weathered sandstone formations which created the Miner's Castle, didn't live up to the pre-trip publicity. Rather, Zach felt that Miner's Castle should have been renamed Queen's Castle and King's Knight, because they looked like pieces from his chess set. The downhill walk, punctuated with several switch-backs, to the observation platform was not without value. A stately pine, that had stood guard over Miner's Castle since the turn of the century, had been struck by lightning. As the surge of electricity hurtled to the ground, the gnarled bark had been completely ripped off in places, exposing narrow vertical strips of pulp wood the length of the entire tree. The majestic pine was trying valiantly to keep it's vigilance, but it's life blood was running in rivulets along the gashes and pooling on the wolmanized deck below. This particular example of nature's destructive power received more of a response from Zach and Taylor than the sculpting prowess of nature at her finest.

The twenty minute drive back to the promised Dairy Queen was not without it's moments. Zachary, thinking about the awesome destructive and creative power of nature came to the following conclusion. "Nature only takes seconds to bust things, but she really takes her time to make things really neat." Bonnie and I just looked at each other .... Maybe we were making progress.

Given a choice between somores and ice cream, and since the boys had somores last night, I voted my 51 per cent and we stopped at the Dairy Queen. Taylor had gotten a rather large soft chocolate filled cone and was having difficulty navigating his way around the badly dripping mound of ice cream. We could trace his progress, or lack of, in the streaks of chocolate in his Point Place T-shirt. The drips started at the Washington Township Fire Department, migrated to Kleis School, turned to the Library, and finally buried themselves in each of Detwiler's eighteen holes.

We always cap off the day with a camp fire, and Sunday was no exception. The fire was carefully planned and executed with the assistance of one crumpled newspaper page, and one wooden safety match. With the flames displaying their shadows on the surrounding pines, Taylor shifted his gaze to the heavens. "Poppa, see that star up there?" Looking in the required vicinity brought a negative response from my part that Taylor just wouldn't accept. Jumping up from his chair, and quickly twisting my head and neck in the required direction, he asked "Now do you see it?" To forestall any further injury, I immediately said yes. To this day I still don't have a clue as to what he wanted me to see, but my neck still hurts when I turn it a certain way.

Bidding farewell to Munising and Grand Island was not without its moments. Early Monday morning Taylor had somehow managed to step on a splinter, and the boys had tried every measure to extract the full grown pine tree. As a last ditch effort, they presented Taylor's injured foot to Poppa for his evaluation. Sometimes with bi-focals the only possible remedy for close work is to remove the glasses entirely, and this delicate operation would require the utmost concentration. Zach was busy gathering the needed extraction tools; and Taylor was already expressing feelings of

Why Can't I Roller Blade in the Grand Canyon

regret when I got my first close look. A small sand thorn had imbedded itself just below Taylor's big toe, and my first attempt at extraction was met with a torrent of tears. The second effort was a total success. Grandma soon had the bandage in place, and the patient was placed in the Jeep's backseat for an extended convalescence.

Taylor and his splinter and the tools required to take it out.

During the drive home down I-75, I asked the boys to recall their favorite activity during the last week. Giving their best thinking imitation, Zach finally allowed that he liked the shipwreck tour the best, and Taylor let it be known that he was partial to ice cream cones, and the bears at the dumpster. However, Zach and Taylor both expressed disappointment over their failure to observe the moose that were clearly pictured on the State of Michigan Highway Map, 1995 edition, along route 41 west of Marquette. When we got back in Toledo, Zach asked me to post a letter for him. It was addressed to then Governor Engler, care of the Michigan Highway Department. *"Dear Sir: About those moose ......*

Why Can't I Roller Blade in the Grand Canyon

The response from "Weekend with Three of the Big Four" has been beyond my expectations. And all kidding aside the humorous sketch has caused some serious discussion with Renee and Jeff. Bonnie and I have always maintained that the childhood days of our kids just dragged, but the years .... Well we just kind of blinked and kids were grown and on their own. We still don't know where the time went. My point being that if you don't spend time with the boys now, there will come a time when they won't want to.

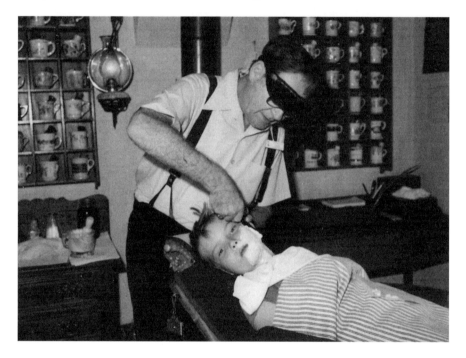

Our son Jeff's first shave.

You know, now that I think about it, my Dad and I had this discussion when I was about Renee's age. Trouble is, ... I'm trying to remember if I listened.

"Dad," Jeff said "why don't you take your newest grandson for the weekend, along with Trevor and Renee's boys, Zach and Taylor? All four of them would enjoy quality time with their grandparents.

Why Can't I Roller Blade in the Grand Canyon

Besides, what's one more?" our son Jeff asked. With a grin on his face, and a wink in his wife's direction, I knew that I was being had. My response, which has long been embedded in the Dickson family lore, was quite predictable, and while Jeff knew what was coming, his wife, Wendy didn't have a clue. "I've never changed a diaper in my entire life, and I see no reason to start with our newest grandson, Kenneth, even if he's my namesake," I responded.

Zach, Trevor, Kenneth, and Taylor in the pool room addition.

At this point in my retirement I really didn't wish to experience one of life's milestones. Bonnie responded with *au contraire,* that I have indeed encountered this initial chapter of fatherhood, and while my response was unconventional, a grandson with a surname of Kenneth did deserve special consideration. What Bonnie

Why Can't I Roller Blade in the Grand Canyon

considered unconventional, I thought was extremely prudent, considering the mental images that were flashing through my mind. With our daughter Renee, I thought little girls were "sugar and spice and everything nice," but a dinner of green beans and blueberry buckle necessitated using the soft spray setting on our family's garden-hose. And as far as Kenneth is concerned, I know what little boys are made of, and the hose didn't have a setting for that.

Trevor and his karate lessons.

Why Can't I Roller Blade in the Grand Canyon

Bonnie and I finished placing Friday's supper on the kitchen table as Zach and Taylor assumed their accustomed seats, and Trevor pushed his chair into place. With the two major religious denominations satisfied after grace, the conversation around the table turned from the last rerun of the "Simpsons" to the boys latest school activities.

Zach and Taylor at the Rainbow's Ice Cream Shop. Porcupine Mountains.

Why Can't I Roller Blade in the Grand Canyon

During a lull in the conversation, Zach with a hint of revenge in his voice, turned toward Taylor and said "Why don't you ask Taylor how he's doing in reading?" Falling into his carefully disguised trap, Bonnie and I both turned to Taylor. Taylor, reacting quickly said "I'm doing ok." Zach, sensing an opening in the game that they both played with increasing intensity, countered with "Really! Then why did Mom have to go and see your teacher?" With a look at his brother that indicated just wait till later, and desperately trying to deflect the focus of conversation, Taylor admitted that reading wasn't up to Mom and Dad's expectations, and that he had to do better.

Sensing a possible "Grand Slam" Zach turned his attention toward Trevor. "Trevor, what did you do in kindergarten today?" Trevor, who had turned into a chatter box since we picked him up from Jeff and Wendy, gave us a complete description of his entire day. From the kid who sits next to him spilling his milk all down the front of his pants, to his buddy that couldn't find his coat, Trevor described every detail of his day in exactly two sentences that totaled twenty-eight words. Not wanting to admit defeat Zach pressed on. "Trevor, you know you have to go back to school on Monday, don't you?' With a look similar to a deer caught in headlights of a fast-moving semi, and his lower lip slightly quivering, he responded "I do?"

With all the dishes safely removed from the table, and the boys trying to decide on tonight's video, Bonnie and I were left alone in the kitchen. "I can't believe it," I said. "What can't you believe," Bonnie asked. "Just before dinner, when the boys were watching Simpson's reruns, Taylor described the whole plot of the episode, and gave Homer's lines perfectly," unbelievable I mumbled. "Why is it that the boys can memorize complete television episodes or song lyrics, and at the same time, have troubles in school," I asked? After teaching for thirty-two years and with kids of our own, I still couldn't put it together. Bonnie, putting down the dish towel and taking my hands in hers, responded "Didn't we have this very conversation, oh, about ten to fifteen years ago, about some other kids that we know? And they turned out all right." I could feel the semi's headlights bearing down on me as we walked out of the

Why Can't I Roller Blade in the Grand Canyon

kitchen.

With the "Clue In The Clock" controversy raging, Nancy Drew, along with the Hardy Boys, were replaced with the video "Little Giants" for the evening's entertainment. Chocolate milk shakes rounded out the late night snacks for the boys. Trevor, vowing to finish his in the morning, snuggled closer to Grandma and was soon asleep

My namesake and Jeff's second son, Kenneth.

Trevor snores in the tradition of Grandpa Baer, and not just a little. Several times during the night I thought the Maumee Bay was being used as a jet landing strip, but the scent of pine chips from the sawmill in the adjoining room belayed the first thought. In the morning, even Zach and Taylor from the relative quiet of the other bedroom, commented on the size of Trevor's woodpile.

Zach, Taylor, Trevor, Kenneth, and Grandma.

Football players from the St. John's "Rebels" and the St. Joan of Arc's "Raiders" were the contestants in this year's clash of titans. Completing the early Saturday morning pep-rally in St. John's parking lot, and with the car properly festooned with the team's colors and slogans, we caravanned with the rest of Point Place, to the University of Toledo's Glass Bowl, the site of this year's Toy Bowl. Taylor, while close to being the smallest Rebel on the team, made up for his shortcomings in stature with grit and determination, and was eagerly awaiting the grid iron contest. Several times during the game, voices boomed from the stands, entreating the coach to put the small guys in. Maybe he didn't hear us, perhaps the game was too close, but "48" never got a chance to turn the game around. All of Taylor's relatives, even Zach, agreed that Taylor could have changed the momentum of the Rebels.

As we left the Glass Bowl, I put a comforting hand on Taylor's slouched shoulders. Trying my best to put a good face on their 38-14 defeat, and drawing inspiration from a similar "Happy Days" episode, I followed Howard Cunningham's example, and offered Taylor several "lifesavers" as we walked to the car. While not being sure of St. Joan of Arc's academic standards for sports, Bonnie and I commented several times on the size of their fifth and sixth graders. Even Zach had never heard of red-shirting fifth graders.

Conversation after dinner again turned to scholastic endeavors. Taylor, recalling Friday's calamity and sensing the turn that the dialogue could take, expertly shifted the discussion to Zach. "Trevor's got about sixteen to twenty years of school to go. How many years do you have to go Zach," Taylor asked? From the hardened glint in Taylor's steely blue eyes, Bonnie and I knew that Zach was being set up, but we couldn't determine from what direction it was coming. Even Trevor was focusing on the give and take. With a quick glance at Taylor, Zach answered "Nine years. Maybe more, four more, that's if I get accepted at a good college." Without giving Zach a chance to take a deep breath Taylor continued. "You will, Bono Tech always needs qualified high school graduates." I was always joking with the boys about the thriving metropolis of Bono and its fine technical school, Bono Tech, but I always assumed they knew I was kidding. Winking in Taylor's direction, I continued with the charade. "Perhaps, if there's time on Sunday, we can visit Bono Tech's campus." Zach's answer was quick and to the point, "Yeah, Right." However, I sensed a hint of uncertainty in his answer. I made tentative plans to pass through Bono on Sunday.

Getting gift ideas from the kids is certainly a lot harder than it used to be. Maybe there are too many toys to choose from, on the other hand, maybe expectations have been raised to record levels. Five, ten dollars in the past used to purchase a neat gift, and you always knew what the kids wanted. Today, fifty to a hundred dollars might purchase the video game, truck, doll or whatever. To that end, we asked the boys what they thought Santa was going to bring them, and what other gifts were still on their list. Ready to check their answers with the respective Mom & Dad, Bonnie and I were prepared to invade the shopping malls in search of the elusive toy.

Mention of Santa; brought knowing laughter from Zach, a look which translated to "you've got to be kidding" from Taylor, and wide eyed wonderment from Trevor. Bonnie, with a quick look at Zach and Taylor, which translated to "don't you dare ruin it for Trevor," both reverted to perfect gentlemen. "Well boys," I intoned, "what's on your wish list this year?"

Toys and stuff tumbled from Trevor faster than he could form the words. He tried to compensate with hand movements and facial features to emphasize the really important items, but he was hopelessly out-classed. Taylor, trying to emulate what he thought his older brother would do, calmly mentioned several video games that would fulfill his Christmas morning expectations. Zach, from the look he gave his brother, indicated that he was way to cool to even contemplate the question.

Trevor was fairly easy. A truck, power ranger, a Disney video and he would enjoy almost anything. And our newest grandchild, Kenneth, would enjoy anything wrapped in Christmas paper, so we weren't really worried about him. However, Zach and Taylor were another quandary. Hearing no serious response to our question, I said "If we don't get some idea of what you two want for Christmas, it's going to be socks and underwear. ...... PINK."

Taylor looked worried, but Zachary, being older and wiser, counseled prudence. With the experience of numerous Christmas mornings under his belt, he privately instructed Taylor and Trevor "Don't worry, they won't do that. It's against the grand-parent's code of conduct."

Todd Petty, our church's minister, has mentioned several times that he noticed Zach and Taylor walking home from St. John's school.

Smiling at the memory, Todd always commented on the boy's deportment. "Zach, with his book bag confidently slung over his shoulder, was always out in front of his brother leading the way home, poised and eagerly awaiting life's next adventure. Taylor, well he's lagging behind his brother, and dragging his book bag by it's remaining frayed strap. His shirt is hanging out, and he has a contented look on his face indicating that he's made it through another day."

Taylor's introduction to trap shooting.

Sunday morning was rather hectic, with four guys and one girl trying to use the same bathroom. With the logistics finally worked out, we found out that Taylor's idea of packing for church was

Why Can't I Roller Blade in the Grand Canyon

baggy sweats and a CYO tee shirt. Taylor, in his haste to participate in Friday's neighborhood football game, forgot to change his school pants. Consequently they required a quick hand washing to remove the grass stains before Bonnie would consider them presentable. The clothes dryer was pressed into emergency service, and a quick trip to the shrinking closet provided Taylor with enough clothes to pass Grandma's inspection.

Trevor learning to fish on the St. Mary's River.

Why Can't I Roller Blade in the Grand Canyon

November finds the elder Dickson serving as the Church's liturgist, and as we arrived Rev. Petty was reintroduced to three of our four grand children. Taking our traditional place in the last pew, the boys eagerly awaited the quick passage of the next hour. After the prelude and before the formal service started, I used the moment to introduce Zach, Taylor, and Trevor to the congregation, and urged everyone to stop and say hi to the boys. Even from the front of the church, I could see the boys planning their revenge.

Waiting for lunch, the boys and I planned the afternoon's activities. The 2.1 mile boardwalk tour through the marshes of Maumee Bay's Little Cedar Point was quickly agreed upon, with a side tour to the observation tower at Crane Creek State Park. As we drove from Maumee Bay to Crane Creek we passed through the thriving metropolis of Bono, and Zach's only remark was "That's Bono?"

Relaxing Sunday night after dropping the boys off, Bonnie and I had a chance to reflect on the weekend's activities. Zach, Taylor, and Trevor had mastered the tactics of tag team wrestling. One would rest while the other two would take over. It was continuous action for the three days, and when they left, Bonnie and I settled in for a long nap.

That action packed weekend triggered another memory of a Sunday several months later when we had the opportunity to take "Three of the Big Four" to the Art Museum.

Sunday afternoon found us with several opportunities to pursue. We gave the boys the choice, and they closed in on the Art Museum. I should explain that part of Saturday's television fare included "The Mummies Curse," and when I pointed out that Toledo's Art Museum had a mummy on display, it was as the kid's say, a done deal.

As we walked through the Museum, the boys asked every guard if we were heading towards the Mummy Room. There were several distractions along the way, but in the end the Egyptian mummy held sway over the "female" statues and paintings. That is, until, they

Why Can't I Roller Blade in the Grand Canyon

found out that the sarcophagus was closed, and that they couldn't see the linen wrapped body. As Zach read the small card explaining that the exhibit was being restored, Taylor was mentally forming the words, "What a Rip!"

We quickly changed directions, and headed for the Cloister, followed by the "Swiss Room," and capped it all off with the story of Rinaldo and Armida from the 16th century poem "Jerusalem Delivered." What an amazing story, but it didn't faze the boys one little bit. However, they were impressed that someone got to paint all over the ceilings and walls of the house without getting into trouble.

The Toledo Museum of Art had a special retrospective of Western Art on display, and last Friday evening was a great time to visit. Even the grandkids thought it was worth the time spent. I was surprised when I asked Zach which painting he thought was the best. Without missing a beat, he said it was Albert Bierstadt's *El Capital, Yosemite Valley, California*. "You know! The big one! Right when you came in the door."

Continuing with our discussion, Zach and I were looking at Albert Bierstadt's *OREGON TRAIL.* The painting is rather large and the detail is amazing. The theme flows from right to left, darkness to light. Starkly present in the dark foreground, just removed from the muddy ruts left by the departing prairie schooners, is a bleached buffalo skeleton in the tall meadow grass. Taken back by the bleached bones, I could see Zach mulling over the possibilities. As his gaze followed the schooner's trek through the valley towards the light in the west, I asked him if he thought the settlers were leaving their old life behind, and heading towards a new life with a fresh beginning. Giving the painting a parting glimpse, Zach turned in my direction. "Of course, Grandpa the bones represent death, the death of two traditional ways of life. The Indians and their lifestyle for one; and second, was scarce jobs and hunger caused by the eastern crop failure which caused many New Englanders to follow their dreams to the beckoning opportunity in the West. The trek through the valley with the steep cliffs on one side and the forbidding forest on the other; signifies darkness to light, and if the migrants would stay on the path of righteousness their salvation was assured. Others might say that it represented the 23rd Psalm.

Zach working in the backyard.

Completely taken back, I couldn't believe this interpretation from the perspective of the seventh grader. "Zach, do you believe that the artist had all this in mind when he started the painting," I asked. Responding, he said "No, I don't think so." "Well then where did you come up with your interpretation of the artist's intent?" With a slight grin forming, Zach continued. "See that lady over there with that group of people? I over heard her say that stuff, as she talked about the painting." With my expanded mental estimation of Zach

Why Can't I Roller Blade in the Grand Canyon

slowly deflating, I quickly came to the conclusion that he thought enough of the explanation to remember it.

What goes around comes around. Renee and Jeff at Four Corners, 1985.

Why Can't I Roller Blade in the Grand Canyon

When Zach first outlined his version of the western adventure at the family's Christmas gathering, I hadn't fully understood the consequences of a 4,831 pound trailer and the Rocky Mountain's highway passes. However, as the gray days of winter slowly gave way to the warm southwesterly breezes of spring, my anxiety level reached new heights as I read and reread the map's tentative mountainous travel route. Zach's Western Adventure 2000, as it was beginning to be called, involved the Air Force Academy, Great Sand Dunes National Monument, Mesa Verde National Park, the south rim of the Grand Canyon, Monument Valley, Arches National Park, and finally the Glacier Basin campground in Rocky Mountain National Park.

Mentally, I recalled the Jeep's sales brochure listing the Cherokee's towing capacity at 5,000 pounds, and in conversations with Jeep's 800 number, the engineers were carefully wording their responses with regards to the almost twelve thousand feet of Colorado's Fall River Pass. And when Renee had "triple A" prepare the "trip tik" for the Western Adventure the almost 12,000' Fall River Pass was coupled with Loveland Pass at 11, 992', Wolf Creek Pass at 10,550', Red Mountain Pass at 11,118', Molas Divide at 10,910', and finally Marsh Pass at 6,550', I was seriously considering a smaller trailer.

With less than a week before the scheduled departure, we opted to make this a true camping adventure, and we substituted the ruggedness of the families 1958 J. C. Higgin's canvas fold-down camper for the comforts afforded by the 23' silver bullet Airstream.

And now as Paul Harvey is fond of saying, "Here's the rest of the story." ....

The arrival of the boys early Monday morning coincided with the first hints of deep orange in the dark eastern sky. We had left room in the tightly packed trailer for the boy's duffel bags, and they were quickly stored along with any last minute toys. While Renee got in several last minute hugs and kisses with the boys, I scanned the dimly lit car interior for anything that looked out of place. What were

Why Can't I Roller Blade in the Grand Canyon

cotton balls doing in the car? ..... Bonnie, why is the Calamine lotion in the car? Rumors of poison ivy had been circulating since the boys returned from their Tobermory camping trip with their Dad, so my questions were strictly rhetorical.

The reddish-yellow hues of dawn illuminated the sleeping forms in the back seat as sunrise caught up with us a little north of Lima. As the boys started struggling with each other for dominance, the complaints of itching coming from the moving forms in the back seat were tied with cries of "what's for breakfast." Both complaints were quickly settled in the McDonald's parking lot near our western course correction. Breakfast specials and Calamine lotion were liberally implemented.

As we inched our way across the Midwest, Taylor kept track of our western progress using the maps of Ohio, Indiana, and Illinois. With the added advantage of the hour's time change, we raced across the Mississippi River and into the fabled St. Louis, the legendary Gateway of the West. Picking our way through the myriad of crowded Interstates, we sighted the St. Louis Arch as the afternoon rush hour formed around us, and like a cresting wave pushed us westward.

We quickly learned the truth of the mythical "Circle of Fire" as our first day journey of 570 miles ended in a KOA campground in Danville, Missouri. Record temperatures followed us west, and all of us were soon soaking wet as our campsite took shape. Our campsite was hidden beneath several tall pines on a slight rise adjacent to an algae covered pond. There were "no fishing" signs posted around its perimeter, but from the wafting foul smell it didn't take us long to determine where the campground's sewage was deposited. Dinner consisted of chicken and noodles followed by a refreshing evening spent in the shade covered swimming pool.

Our first western sunset was obscured by a heavy evening haze which dampened the little breeze that strayed through the trees. Sweating into the night, all of us tossed and turned through our first night on the road, as we tried to find a restful position. Towards morning, Zach's quest for the perfect sleeping position caused the aged green canvas of his cot to fail, depositing Zach unceremoniously on the floor. And to make matters worse, muffled giggles emanated from the lump in the adjacent cot.

Zach and Grandma trying to repair Zach's ripped canvas cot.

As the day progressed, the gray morning fog slowly lifted revealing the tree lined hills of Missouri's interior. Continuing our western trek on I-70, the temperature kept pace with our mileage, as we worked our way towards the Missouri River and Independence. As we traveled the interstate through Harry Truman's Independence, the skyline of Kansas City was perfectly framed in the elliptical arch of an overpass. With the reflecting sunlight, the modern buildings of downtown Kansas City looked liked the fabled "Emerald City" of L. Frank Baum's tome, *The Wonderful Wizard of Oz.*" Could the four of us have been on the "Yellow Brick Road?" with Grandma obviously fitting the part of Dorothy. The boys and I spent the better part of the afternoon trying to decide who was the Tin Man, the Scare Crow, and the Cowardly Lion. As to Toto, the dog never came up.

The temperature was supposed to increase to over 100 degrees in eastern Kansas, and from a quick glance at the Jeep's temperature gage, I think we were way past that. With the car's air conditioning functioning at peak performance, we traveled through the afternoon stopping at a private campground in WaKeeney, Kansas. As we registered for the night, the proprietor from the cool recesses of the log cabin's counter, proudly indicated that yesterday's 115 degrees wouldn't be repeated. Continuing "Yep, you're really lucky, the heat wave finally broke, it's only going to be 93 degrees tonight." Seconds turned to minutes, as he considered the proper campsite for our canvas covered trailer. The shade trees next to the ripening soy beans beckoned the Higgins, and we settled on campsite number 34. The needle and thread repair of Zach's canvas cot occupied a little more than an hour before dinner, which left the ample after dinner evening hours to enjoy the inviting waters of the shade covered pool. The surrounding country-side was illuminated with the brilliant colors of the high plains, and the crystal waters of the pool reflected the deep hues of sunset as another day drifted away. Well, ... somebody had to do it.

During the night I felt myself being bitten in the neck by some sort of bug, and without further thought on my part, I squashed the bug between my fingers and threw it into the night. As the squashed bug curved into the darkness, I remembered my last image of Zach before we turned out the battery powered light. Zach was carefully positioned on his back, trying to avoid the repaired tear in his cot, and peacefully snoring with his mouth wide open. Listening for the bug as it arched towards Zach's sleeping form, I heard the bug hit the canvas side wall of the trailer, and then silence. I asked him during breakfast the next morning if he dreamed about eating any new foods last night. Zach looked at me like I was crazy, and he replied, "No ... he didn't think so, but he really didn't recall." Taylor, knowing about the bug, looked all over that trailer as he packed up the cots and sleeping bags, but he never did find that squashed bug.

Taylor and Zach watch as the Jeep is winched upon the flatbed.

It was late morning when the scrub trees of Colorado's eastern high plains gave way to the rapidly growing city of Colorado Springs. Perched on the eastern side of the Rocky Mountain's Pike National Forest, we followed US 24 into the heart of the city. Maneuvering through the heavy noon traffic we heard and felt a huge bang, then

Why Can't I Roller Blade in the Grand Canyon

silence, followed by the Jeep's warning light illuminating the "check gages." Initially unable to comprehend what had happened, I noticed the temperature gage rapidly edging its way towards 250 degrees. I brought the injured car to a stop amidst three lanes of increasingly maddening traffic. It was evident as I pulled into the nearest parking area that the power steering and brakes had failed. Previous conditioning with our Camaro in the Western States, directed my next actions, I called Chrysler road side assistance at 1.800.521.2779.

The towing company was on the scene within the hour, and after some initial confusion as to the disposition of the camping trailer, we were taken to a Jeep Dealership. With the Jeep Cherokee firmly attached to the flatbed of the wrecker and the Higgin's hooked to the truck's hitch, there was no room for us to ride in the cab. Consequently after further discussion, we rode in the Jeep to the dealership. Firmly buckled in, our newly combined height, coupled with two independent suspensions, gave us the ride of a "Monster Truck" as we pitched and rolled with each twist and turn of the street. Zach and Taylor enjoyed the ride, Bonnie and I thought about the soothing effects of Dramamine.

Our arrival at the dealership was not without its moments. The dealership's Service Writer was not confident in his ability to immediately repair the damage. His response was "we're extremely busy, and I don't think we can even look at your car today. If I were you, I would plan on at least three days in Colorado Springs." Mulling over his casual response to our predicament, Zach and I came up with a great plan.

I'm not quite sure how the Jeep dealer arrived at the conclusion that I was writing a feature article for *Jeeper's* magazine about our Western Adventure, but the laptop and Zach's well timed questions brought forth the desired result. I certainly wasn't going to correct their impressions.

The water pump, pulley, serpentine belt and fan blade assembly all had to be replaced, and by closing time we were on our way. It's

Why Can't I Roller Blade in the Grand Canyon

amazing how we went from three days to repair, to three hours. We hooked up the trailer, said thank you, and headed into the mountains and the campground at Cripple Creek. Rather than complicate matters with dinner, we filled the gas tank and headed west on US 24. It was almost 7:30 our time when we arrived at the last campsite in the National Forest campground. Calling it a campsite at 10,000 feet is being kind and generous, and as we looked it over, the heavens opened up with a torrential downpour. Bonnie and I struggled to set the trailer up in the rain, and without wood to block the wheels it was quite a balancing act. The heavy rain made the hard pan clay extremely slippery, and with every part of the site's terrain heading down hill, we thought that the site was precarious at best. Exertion at about 9375 feet is never a good idea, but I was never one to let a little thing like oxygen slow me down. We got the camp set up in the downpour, and I walked downhill to the ranger station for wood to block the tires, and then ran back up to the campsite with an armload of suitable wheel chocks.

With the camp somewhat in order, attention was now directed towards dinner. Zach and Taylor, who had been in the car up to this point, were now doing what all kids do when they are hungry, complain. With an increase in the wind and rain, the cafe (Wendys) in Woodland Park was a much better solution to dinner than the Coleman camp stove.

Dashing through the deepening puddles in the parking lot, Zach and Taylor jostled each other for position at the counter. Waiting for Taylor to complete his order, Zach was over-heard to tell the cashier that he was so hungry; his stomach thought his throat had been cut. The cashier must have heard all this before because her demeanor didn't change when she got to us. While the boys finished their chicken nuggets, french fries, chocolate milk shakes, and my cheeseburger, Bonnie's attention was drawn to my shortness of breath, and gray coloring. The tingling sensation in my hands had increased, and the dizzy nauseated feeling I was experiencing necessitated a quick trip to the men's room.

Why Can't I Roller Blade in the Grand Canyon

I spent about two hours at the Urgent Care Center hooked up to oxygen to counter the effects of the altitude, and at the same time medication was administered to bring my blood pressure down. The doctor, conferring with Dr. Mom and the boys, thought it would be a good idea if we were to spend the night in Colorado Springs at a much lower altitude. Unbeknownst to me, Bonnie and the boys had driven back to the rain drenched campground, and in the dwindling evening light, packed up the gear and trailer. And like Clark and Ellen Griswold's Aunt Edna, I was released from the Urgent Care, and in the pouring rain strapped to the Jeep's roof rack for the trip back down the canyon to the motel.

The Colorado Springs Howard Johnson's was just what Dr. Mom ordered. The boys caught up with several of their television programs, while I enjoyed the comforts of a Queen size bed. The sunrise was about 8:30 our time, 6:30 theirs, and with the Wheaties came a stern lecture from my traveling companions. They all chimed in, "Don't over do it."

Zach and Taylor at the entrance to the Air Force Academy.

Our next destination was the Air Force Academy. Arriving at the main gate we asked what we thought were intelligent questions as we tried not to disappoint the guard on duty. However Taylor had his own agenda and was bound and determined to tell the guard all about the students that his Grandpa had sent to the Academy. As Taylor caught his breath, Zach asked the guard if he knew Poppa's former students. Carefully measuring his response to the boys, the guard explained that his military police unit was not allowed to visit with the students, but he would be happy to take a couple of photos of the boys at the entrance if they wanted. With the gray concrete and steel Air Force emblem in the background, and with the boys playing the perfect tourists, the uniformed sentinel snapped off several frames. Thanking him for his courteous actions, we bid farewell to Airman Anderson, as he once again explained the travel directions.

On the grounds of the Air Force Academy.

The fifteen minute drive through the evergreen dotted foothills brought us to the Visitor Center as they opened their doors for the day's tourists. We caught the informative 14 minute film, and

Why Can't I Roller Blade in the Grand Canyon

followed the knowledgeable tour guide for the half mile walk to the Cadet Chapel. Even though Bonnie and I had visited the Chapel almost twenty years earlier, the same awe-inspiring feelings rose to the surface, as the subdued sunlight passed through the multi-colored window glass and danced across the walnut pews of the main chapel.

The boys were impressed and at the same time awed by the Chapel. They listened closely as the guide explained why the cross leaned forward, and when she discussed the number of pipes in the wind driven organ they retreated in disbelief. Zach and Taylor placed themselves on each side of the chapel and began to count the pipes in an effort to keep the guide honest, but were distracted from their task when she mentioned that the smallest pipe was the size of a ball point pen.

The Air Force Academy's Chapel.

Why Can't I Roller Blade in the Grand Canyon

The immense size of the Chapel's seventeen spires was contrasted with the workmen resealing parts of the aluminum roof sheeting. One of the tour group asked the guide if there was any significance to the 17 spires. With a quick smile that highlighted her youth she replied, "Why they represent the 12 Apostles and the 5 Joint Chief's of Staff."

Sun-shades in the form of covered wagons over the picnic tables.

Driving south on I-25 after lunching at the Air Force Academy, we thought that Pueblo State Park would meet our expectations for the night. Our campsite overlooked the front range of the eastern Rockies west of the Pueblo Reservoir. In the High Plains, trees are scarce and dwarfed by the harsh climate, and the only shade offered is from the "covered wagon" canopies that screen the picnic tables from the sun.

All day long the western mountains had been highlighted by threatening thunder clouds, and the resulting rain bursts were being pushed north, parallel to the eastern range, by the heat of the surrounding barren country. Glimpses of lightning striking the Rocky Mountains illuminated the evening sky, and were in stark contrast to the palate of blues gracing the eastern sky. As the ferocious lightning followed by distant thunder boomed and danced across the peaks of the San Isabel National Forest, sunset brought us the black skies and wind gusts of childhood memories.

From the safety of our sheltered campfire, the boys were drawn into the beauty of the contrasts, and were mesmerized by the majesty of Nature's natural fireworks. Sensing a moment that will never be repeated, I asked the boys what they were thinking about. Zach, looking at Taylor for confirmation and choosing his response carefully, "Poppa .... you remember that Dairy Queen when we came into the campground? Can we get a couple of smoothies?" As I looked into their faces the sublime and celebrated moment had gone astray like the storm that had vanished into the evening's twilight. The smoothies were excellent.

Entering the Great Sand Dunes National Monument from the south, the refreshing fragrance of the Pinion trees wafting across the High Desert was in stark contrast to the pungency escaping from the burned over sections of forest that were interspersed with the beginnings of the dunes. The campsites while spacious, are contained with capped field stone knee walls, and surrounded with mature Pinion trees. The result of the campsite arrangement enhances your experience in the park. If you place your tent correctly, the picnic table gives you a great view of the Colorado sunsets and the magnificent sand dunes.

Notices placed in strategic locations throughout the park warned visitors of mountain lion and bear visits during the early and late hours of the day. When we registered, the ranger had stressed the need to place all foodstuffs in the car when not in use. We walked all through the park, and while there were numerous reports from fellow campers, we didn't have a single confirmed sighting.

Taylor, Grandpa, and Grandma at the Great Sand Dunes entrance.

The boys wanted to climb to the top of the dunes, and at 8200' I was not about to risk that kind of a climb. Using the informational pamphlets that the Park's Visitor Centers were noted for, we decided on a hike that would follow a dried up creek bed that paralleled the dune base. The surface temperature of the dunes was approaching 140 degrees as we started out on our mid-morning walk. We passed several boys carrying "super sized" skateboards. Zach and Taylor quickly corrected my error, "Grandpa, they're called Boogie Boards." As Taylor continued the explanation, I found out that the boards were designed for downhill dune surfing. The nature walk took on new urgency as the boys looked for the Boogie Board's rental booth. They didn't find it, and Bonnie and I were both relieved.

Why Can't I Roller Blade in the Grand Canyon

That evening we attended a nature program at the Visitor Center funded by the "Friends of the Dunes," that was capped by a beautiful sunset.

Taylor in the desolation of the Great Sand Dunes

Leaving the Great Sand Dunes and the Sangre De Cristo Range of the Rocky Mountains behind, we continued to follow United States route 160 west. The High Plains faded as pine covered mountains crowded in on the once broad valley as we were drawn towards Wolf Creek Pass. At 10,850' it gave the boys a new respect for the Colorado Rockies. Pagosa Springs arrived as we literally flew down the twists and turns of the San Juan Mountains. Arriving at noon our time the McDonalds was still serving breakfast. While Bonnie and I have long since passed on the boys taste in foods, the couple next to us took umbrage with Zach's lemonade and egg McBiscuit. And when Taylor arrived with a chocolate shake and sausage McMuffin they decided it was time to leave. However, they were overheard saying "that's another reason we shouldn't eat at fast food restaurants."

Climbing rapidly out of the Animas River Valley, Durango was quickly left behind as we entered the San Juan National Forest. The boys were amazed as the mountain tops leveled off, and the terrain settled into broad river valleys confined by massive plateaus. Leaving the post office in Mancos behind us, I knew it wasn't long till we entered Mesa Verde National Park.

Taylor, Grandpa, and Grandma at Mesa Verde National Park.

The swift climb from the floor of the Mancos River valley to the mesa top afforded some spectacular views of the Ute Mountain Range to the west. Checking in at Moorefield Village, our reservations were soon located, and we were given the option of choosing our own campsite. The campground's scrub oak afforded little shade as we searched for the perfect site. Relief from the late afternoon sun was a decided plus, and the trailer and tarp were placed to achieve the desired result. The picnic table did not lend itself to our plan, and when we tried to move it a rather flimsy chain held it firmly in place. A couple of well placed tugs coupled with an

Why Can't I Roller Blade in the Grand Canyon

errant screw driver, and the table was properly placed. Zach was worried that the picnic table police would stumble upon our crime, and that we would all be placed in custody. Taylor, on the other hand, said "only Poppa would go to picnic table jail. After all, he did it." It wasn't long before the picnic table story entered into the written records of the Woods Expedition.

With the picnic table firmly under the shade of the tarp, dinner's underway.

We tried to get to the Far View Visitor Center before they adjourned for the evening, but dinner and dishes pushed our arrival past their closing time. However, the twisting 13 mile drive to the Center afforded us great panoramic vistas to view the rainstorms as they raced across the Montezuma Valley. Mesa Verde was in dire need of rain, and the fire crews were on constant call to extinguish the numerous fires resulting from the random lightning strikes within the Park's perimeter. Zach noticed a small gathering of park employees talking about a group of fire fighters in the National Park that are called "hot shots." "They are dropped at the fire's location in the park by helicopter, and they stay there till it's out. Can you imagine that," Zach asked?

One of the rest areas and overlooks in Mesa Verde.

Walking back to the car, and as if in answer to the Park's prayers, it started to pour. As we exited the parking lot, little wisps of steam were rapidly forming on the Park's black asphalt roads. The rain quickly passed, and we were rewarded with an immense double rainbow that seemed to follow the mesa south. In an adjacent field, the stunted grass stubble held on to the precious drops of rain, and when the sun returned, the entire field came alive with the brilliance of thousands of sparkling diamonds. Our next stop was the Park's headquarters at Spruce Tree House.

Daylight was rapidly vanishing, and across from our campsite, the rain obscured sunset had disappeared behind the mesa. The boys were using the time to catch up on their correspondence, and Bonnie and I were just reflecting upon the days activities. "Boys, boys," I softly said, "be extremely quiet, and no fast moves. Look at the deer moving through the scrub oak." Gathering confidence as they moved down the slight open hill, four females and a buck nibbled at the white flowering grasses that covered the open field behind our campsite. It was almost dark when the boys finished their letters and called it a day.

The darkness that enveloped the mesa hid the gathering storms from view, and when they struck the Higgins, it reminded me of an old dog worrying a new bone. The rain was being driven in horizontal sheets, and several times the wind gusts gave us flight. Throughout the raging storm the boys never woke up, and the rainstorm sensing failure, doubled its efforts to dislodge our tent stakes and wake the boys. We greeted the first rays of sunrise with wet canvas and warm sleeping bags. As we prepared breakfast and detailed our plans for the day, the gathering sunrise quickly chased away the early morning gloom.

In early April we decided to enhance Zach and Taylor's visit to the Anasazi ruins on the Wetherill's Mesa. After reading all the travel brochures, we arranged for an enlightened counselor to guide our ramblings through Mesa Verde. Sunday morning caught us kidding each other as we hiked to the pre-arranged pick-up location at Morefield Village. We were still laughing about the similarities to the Gilligan's Island theme ...... *"Just sit right back, and let me tell you a tale of a three hour tour"*...and our eight hour jaunt as the guide's van engine sputtered to life.

Our guide's name was Peggy, and after the required small talk and introductions, she asked several questions to determine our interest and knowledge level. Taking the lead, Zach answered her questions, while at the same time inserting several of his own. Visibly impressed, Zach's graduate course in Anasazi Culture commenced as we arrived at the Far View Complex. From that point on, Peggy concentrated on enhancing Zach's overall understanding and opinion of the early southwest Indian culture. And, as for the rest of us, we just kind of tagged along.

As we approached the chuck wagon, Zach and Taylor jockeyed for positions as they ran across the gravel parking lot. Taylor, barely clearing a low scrub evergreen, won the impromptu foot race for the chow line. Rewarding Taylor's prowess, the cook gave him the leather covered black metal bar and told him to vigorously strike the chuck wagon's triangular gong. Although Taylor had won the race, during lunch Zach managed to get in the last word. Taylor had dribbled barbeque sauce all over his shirt, and Zach responded with "Taylor, there's another couple of items you can add to your shirt's food collection." Looking at our table's companions and then back to Zach, Taylor said "that's a snack for later." We scored it a tie, but our lunch companions gave the exchange to Zach. At the end of the day both boys had earned the Mesa Verde National Park's Junior Warden's Badge.

Zach and Taylor grinding corn the Anasazi way.

The Silverton & Durango Railroad has dominated the town of

Durango, Colorado for the better part of a hundred years now, and a visit to the turn of the century depot is a must on any western trip. Our arrival into the town was considerably later than we had planned. Terrific thunderstorms had raked the Mesa Verde during the night, and our campground had not escaped nature's tantrum. We heard the "thump, thump, thump," of the helicopters as the park's "hotshots" were called out to extinguish the random lightning strikes. Our tarp, while stretched and pocketed with pools of rain water, had survived, but our neighbor's tent had collapsed during the height of the storm. The deluge had drenched their gear and forced them into the car to await the dawn.

Taylor, Zach, and Grandma on the overlook back to Far View.

The twisting road off the mesa revealed the accidental deaths of several mountain lion cubs and a couple of other animals common to the scrub of the mesas'. Peggy told us earlier that the animals sleep on the black top roads to conserve their energy by absorbing the heat from the roads, and that it's a harsh park problem.

The Silverton & Durango RR and all the things to get into.

The Silverton & Durango Roundhouse provided the boys with a glimpse into the early workings of the Nation's railroads. Several steam engines were in the rebuilding process, and the technicians were eager to answer the boy's questions. The Museum detailed the growth of the line, and provided hands-on exhibits that encouraged exploration. While Zach was exploring the controls of a narrow gage 2-6-2 steam engine, Taylor was investigating the innards of the engine's firebox and grate. Bonnie and I caught up with the boys as they held on to the brass rail that paralleled the narrow side boards as they inched along the length of the engine. Their intended destination, before the museum guard spotted their activities, was the atypical smokestack and polished brass bell above the unique "cow catcher."

Who's stronger?

Taylor at "Four Corners."

Why Can't I Roller Blade in the Grand Canyon

The acrid smell of wood smoke from the numerous forest fires hung in the air, as we returned to our campsite high on the mesa. The deer still traveled through the park's campsites, but their seemingly cavalier attitude was replaced with weariness as they constantly sniffed the air drafts that coursed down the valley. Statuesque hummingbirds constantly tried to withdraw nectar as they hovered between the red flowers on Bonnie's dish towels, As we planned our next day's journey across the "Four Corner's" area of the Ute Mountain Indian Reservation, the boys were disappointed that they hadn't seen the mountain lions and the bear cubs that had been reported in our part of the park.

Zach has another way of being in all four states at the same time.

The drive from Mesa Verde to Grand Canyon is still 290 miles of nothing, interspersed with more of nothing. The highlight of the early morning is our stop at the "Four Corners." While the boys showed complete disdain at our suggestion of placing feet and hands in each of the four states, as soon as they were out of the car they did just that. Photographs were quickly taken to record the event, and it wasn't long before we were crossing the Chuska Mountains as we skirted Monument Valley. Kayenta loomed on the horizon of the Black Mesa area, and after 137 miles lunch and gas were in order. Kayenta now has a newly constructed shopping center adjacent to the fast food restaurants, Burger King and McDonalds. Compared to our last visit, it looks like the place is growing by leaps and bounds. When the boys had to pay for a glass of water, it drove home the point the area's growth is only constrained by a lack of water. Following US 160 west, our arrival at Tuba City, was continually delayed by constant road construction.

The gray washes of the red rock of Echo Cliffs soon gave way to the beginnings of Arizona's Painted Desert. The suspension bridge of an oil pipeline, announced our westward turn at Cameron, for the Grand Canyon. Climbing towards the forests of Kaibab National Forest, the desert scrub was soon left behind. The "Arrowhead" symbol of the National Parks announced our arrival at Desert View, and while we waited our turn for the required pictures, the boys were talking with a couple of kids from Vermont.

What a surprise Mom & Fred at the Grand Canyon.

We had almost another hour's drive through the Ponderosa Pine forest before we arrived at our campground in the Grand Canyon Village. The first campsite we were assigned was framed perfectly among the mature pines, but we were unable to set the tent stakes before we struck impenetrable stone inches below the surface. Bonnie waited till the boys put on their roller blades, and walked back to the ranger station with her wheeled escorts. After explaining the situation we were fortunate enough to get another site that met our requirements. The heat has been oppressive and the shade afforded by our tarp has been essential to enjoy the surroundings of the Aspen Campground.

Second campsite in Grand Canyon's Aspen Campground.

Unbeknownst to the boys, Renee and Fred had flown into Las Vegas earlier in the day, rented a convertible, and were driving across the Northwest corner of Arizona for a much planned surprise at the Grand Canyon. Consequently, the boys didn't understand why we were hanging around the campsite, when the much talked about Grand Canyon beckoned. While the boys roller bladed on the asphalt campsite loops, checking in on every lap, we waited in the

Why Can't I Roller Blade in the Grand Canyon

shade for their arrival. Towards mid-afternoon a bright blue Mustang convertible pulled into our campsite as the boys glided in behind it .... speechless. They had just talked to their Mom on the phone last night and didn't believe what they were seeing. While I was saying "who the hell is that?" Zach interrupts, and says "it looks like Mommy and Fred, but it can't be." They quickly recovered, and showered Renee with hugs and kisses and Fred with high fives. For the next hour, it was one question after another as the boys relived their western adventure, and grilled Renee and Fred as to how they kept their travel plans secret. The reunion continued through dinner, and Fred was later heard to remark "I've flown 2300 miles for this gathering, and I was rewarded with chicken and noodles for dinner."

While we didn't have the deer ranging through the campsite as we did at Mesa Verde, we have seen white tail deer walking through the campsite. The perfect setting for the park's coyotes to serenade each other is in the small hours of the morning. One coyote starts to call, and before long, others from all the points of the compass were joining in. They must have kept at it for an hour or so, and then only the call of the raven interrupted the stillness of the night.

Zach and Taylor have completed their Junior Parks Ranger program here at the Grand Canyon. While much of the written questions pertained to the park itself, they had to complete an ecology project suited to their age. With Fred and Renee helping, Zach and Taylor had to clear a field of tumbleweed growth. It seems the plant, while prominently displayed in all the western movies, it is only native to Russia, and the park's plan is to remove it completely.

Grand Canyon Village is almost overrun with cars and trucks of every size and description including Zach and Taylor on roller blades. Traffic is routed through the park with a road system similar to the interstate, complete with clover leafs, that move tourists from one overlook to the next. Park officials have developed a bus loop system, and closed the outer drives to all but the propane powered trams. Through experience, we found that early morning, is the best

Why Can't I Roller Blade in the Grand Canyon

time to visit the prominent vantage points along the southern rim. The bus drivers are still friendly, and the tourists are sparse.

Taylor working on his written "Junior Ranger" program.

A short 5 minute walk is all that's required to take us to the

Canyon's south rim and the Bright Angel overlook. Zach and Taylor promised to remove their roller blades once we got to the rim trail and replace them with their walking shoes. The asphalt covered path is at times right on the edge of the canyon, and the unrestricted views that are afforded, are magnificent. I understood why we were the center of attention when I noticed that Taylor hadn't removed his roller blades as promised. Our other companions on the Grand Canyon rim trail parted as Taylor flew by oblivious to the dangers just a heartbeat away. His new found adventure was ended almost as soon as it began, and when his mother finished explaining the dangers of his foolish act, I started using entirely different words. After changing into his shoes and catching up with Zach, Taylor was heard to remark *"I don't know why I can't roller blade in the Grand Canyon."*

Grandma, Zach, & Renee walking on the Grand Canyon Rim trail.

Fred's reluctance to view the Canyon's depths from anything but a healthy distance from the edge should have been the signal that he

Why Can't I Roller Blade in the Grand Canyon

was challenged by heights. Renee knew of his difficulty, but he had sworn her to secrecy. The boys and I kept urging Fred to enjoy the same vistas that we were observing, but it wasn't till Fred took me aside, and explained his hesitance, that I fully understood. Now I understand why he wanted to take all the group shots with the Grand Canyon as the back drop.

Zach and Taylor next to the 4 – 6 – 2 "Pacific" steam engine and its 6 foot drivers.

Renee and Fred, with the boys firmly in tow, had taken the tram to Hermit's Rest at the end of the outer western loop. This gave Bonnie and I a chance to visit the Grand Canyon Art Retrospective in the often used lecture hall of the Kolb Studio. Located at the head of the Bright Angel Trail, the studio is perched precariously on the Canyons very edge. While the resulting vistas are breath taking, it does give one pause. The exhibit of Grand Canyon Art had taken over three years to assemble; resulting in views of the Canyon through eyes of such talented artists was certainly wonderment. As the afternoon hour approached three, we heard the train's steam whistle announce its approaching departure. We have heard the shrill whistle of the 4-8-2 Atlantic steam engine of the Grand Canyon Railway every day at noon as it pulls into the cedar trimmed station below the El-Tovar Hotel. Today, the steam whistle beckoned us to explore the train before it pulled away from the station on its return to Williams. Our senses were rewarded as we watched the engine transfer its power to the six foot drive wheels. The huge steel wheels in unison slipped and grappled for traction on the shiny rails. As the train headed for high desert of the Coconino Plateau, it sure was a thrill to see it shouldering the twenty restored Pullmans and observation cars. You had to look for them, but hidden between the two water tenders were several diesel engines disguised as boxcars for added power.

By the end of the day, all of us had walked several miles, so when I suggested that we view the coming sunset, there weren't many takers. With the dinner, dishes, and correspondence behind us, the late evening walk to the Canyon's edge at Yavapai Point was well attended. With our departure scheduled for early the next morning, we were all rewarded with one of the Grand Canyon's most spectacular sunsets.

When Renee and Fred left for their return flight home, we had three very sad boys, and it wasn't a very good afternoon. It has been exceptionally hot, and for the three days we've been here the temperature has been in the mid nineties with very little air. The rangers have advised no hiking activity between 10 and 4, so we got into the car to explore the Watchtower and the museum at the park's eastern entrance. With kind words to explain their feelings, the boys felt better by the evening's campfire program. The nights have been fairly pleasant, hovering in the mid fifties, and are a welcome respite to the hot days.

By the way, Zach's cot had ripped again, only this time it was not repairable. We snickered at his misfortune, but no one dared to say that Zach had a lead butt. However, Taylor was overheard later in the day voicing what everyone was thinking. After much thought, we gathered the entire family together at the dumpster, and with all the dignity that we could muster for the occasion ..... Zach's cot was given a proper dumpster burial after a solemn ceremony. Zach and Taylor after saying a few words, very carefully tossed the frame and its tattered green canvas cloth in the dumpster.

The car is giving me pause again. When the air conditioning is activated, the serpentine drive belt rebels with a horrible screeching sound. From past experience, that sound usually indicates a loose belt, and with today's cars that means a trip to the dealer. The closest Jeep dealer was in Flagstaff ..... 84 miles from the campground, and the other one was in Cortez ... 290 miles. So we headed for Flagstaff. The dealership was so small that they didn't even have a new car in stock. Anyway, the mechanic decided that the belt was incorrectly tensioned, and as a result could have flown off at anytime during our trek. We have decided to head for Phoenix and our friends the Hallins. I've talked to a Jeep dealer, and he advised us to continue the vacation and enjoy the view. His parting words were "don't have a heart attack." Easy for him to say.

While the dealer's technician properly tensioned the drive belt, Bonnie caught the latest western news on CNN. It seems that our plans to return to the Rocky Mountains through Cortez and Mesa Verde must be set aside. Forest fires have closed the Four Corner area and Mesa Verde National Park. Further details revealed that Morefield Campground, had been totally burned over, by a rapidly moving forest fire. Instead of heading north to Cortez and Mesa Verde, our revised travel plans now included a visit with Mitch & Macy Hallin in Phoenix, The two-hour drive to Phoenix, down I-17 at the legal speed, with the air conditioner functioning, proved to be a pretty good test drive for the belt's tension.

Why Can't I Roller Blade in the Grand Canyon

The boys were in the height of their glory. Mitch and Macy had a backyard pool, and the boys were making up for lost time. Mitch is an excellent cook and breakfast was always an adventure. This morning's repast was no exception as Mitch asked the boys what they would like to do. When the boys couldn't arrive at a decision, Mitch suggested a late lunch at Cooper's Town, a well known sports bar in downtown Phoenix. Mitch knew the owner Vince Furnier and maybe the boys would get to meet him.

The cool interior of Cooper's Town was highlighted with specially designed cases of pro-sports memorabilia hung from the walls and tastefully intermingled between the tables. Zach and Taylor were in awe as they were drawn from one display to the next. Many of their seasonal sports heroes were represented in the displays of basketball, football, hockey, and baseball. The boys were on their third journey through the displays when Mitch asked them if they would like to meet the owner. Mr. Furnier arrived at our table dressed in tan slacks and a light blue polo shirt. As Mitch introduced each of the boys to Alice Cooper, they rose, shook hands, and then introduced Grandma and Grandpa.

They were extremely polite but both of them refused to believe that they had just met THE Alice Cooper. Later, Taylor was overheard to say to his brother, "I've seen pictures of Alice Cooper .... And that's not him." On the other hand Zach being older and wiser said to his brother "You know, it might have been. I wondered why the cards said Enjoy, Vince "Alice Cooper" Furnier."" After dinner that evening both of the boys asked Mr. Hallin "Was that really Alice Cooper?" The look on the boy's faces was priceless as Mitch and Macy stole glances at each other and started laughing.

According to Friday's USA Today, 500 acres were burned in less than three hours, as authorities evacuated over 1,500 visitors and campers from Mesa Verde National Park. If we would have continued with our original travel plans we would have been right in the middle of that mess.

You have often heard the economics expression "supply and

demand." Well Zach has taken that simple expression and fine tuned it for his own use. According to his interpretation it goes something like this; "I demand that you supply me with ice cream." After dinner Saturday night, Zach finally got his wish, but after an excellent Mexican repast he was either too full or too tired to accept.

The early afternoon was spent looking into the wares of several used book stores. One of the stores that we visited had an excellent collection of Michigan material. Several of the items which I've never seen before, really peaked my interest. Bonnie said to purchase them if I wanted, but with 2,000 miles of travel till we reached home, I decided to pass.

We have also heard that the forest fire at Mesa Verde is still out of control, and that there is another fire twenty or so miles west of Cortez. Both fires were started by lightning and are burning out of control. Mitch had mapped out our return to the interstate so that we could fully appreciate the Mogollon Rim. Coming up from Phoenix on US 87, after leaving Payson, we could see distant black smoke smudges from the forest fires on the horizon. By the time we got to Holbrook on Arizona highway 377, we could see the smoke spiraling towards the forming thunder heads in the early morning sky.

After two long days on the road home, Zach was overheard passing on the following insight to his brother. "Taylor we're having a serious crisis! We're out of batteries," cried Zach. With due consideration and a concerned look, Taylor replied "Since we can't play with our game boys, we'll just have to go home."

I hope that you have enjoyed the telling of the tale of this vacation. Bonnie and I have often wondered if the boys enjoyed themselves. Our reply came late in the third day of our homeward journey as we were approaching Defiance, Ohio. Zach was overheard asking Taylor ....."I wonder where we're going next year." At that point it was all worth it ...... Life's good.

Why Can't I Roller Blade in the Grand Canyon

Renee's travelers: Zach & Taylor.

Zach, Mechanical Engineering, University of Toledo.

Taylor, Recruit, United States Marine Corp.

Or son Jeff's future story tellers: Trevor, Derrick, Kenneth, and Adrianna.

Bonnie and I hope that every family has at least one member who remembers the story's that make their family unique and special. As long as those family members are remembered and their contributions are treasured, they will always be with us.